W9-AHH-922

marketing strategies
for the home-based business

HOME-BASED BUSINESS SERIES

marketing strategies for the home-based business

Solutions You Can Use Today

Shirley George Frazier

Guilford, Connecticut

This book's purpose is to provide accurate and authoritative information on the topics covered. It is sold with the understanding that neither the author nor the publisher is engaged in rendering legal, financial, accounting, and other professional services. Neither The Globe Pequot Press nor the author assumes any liability resulting from action taken based on the information included herein. Mention of a company name does not constitute endorsement.

To buy books in quantity for corporate use
or incentives, call **(800) 962–0973**
or e-mail **premiums@GlobePequot.com.**

Copyright © 2008 by Shirley George Frazier

All rights reserved. No part of this book may be reproduced or transmitted in any form by any means, electronic or mechanical, including photocopying and recording, or by any information storage and retrieval system, except as may be expressly permitted by the 1976 Copyright Act or by the publisher. Requests for permission should be made in writing to The Globe Pequot Press, P.O. Box 480, Guilford, Connecticut 06437.

Text design: Nancy Freeborn

Library of Congress Cataloging-in-Publication Data

Frazier, Shirley George.
  Marketing strategies for the home-based business : solutions you can use today / Shirley George Frazier. — 1st ed.
    p. cm. — (Home-based business series)
  ISBN-13: 978-0-7627-4240-0
  1. Home-based businesses—Marketing. 2. Marketing. 3. Success in business. I. Title.
  HD62.38.F73 2008
  658.8'02--dc22

                                                              2007042322

Manufactured in the United States of America
First Edition/First Printing

To my mom and my husband, John, who support and encourage me through every marketing challenge, no matter what the outcome. A special thanks to my editor, Paula Brisco, for making easy work of difficult tasks.

Contents

Introduction | xi

What Qualifies Me to Be Your Mentor | xii

How This Book Is Organized | xv

Caveats to Consider as You Start | xvi

01   Your Marketing Plan—The First Step to Success | 1

Marketing Plan No. 1: Product Business | 2

Marketing Plan No. 2: Service Business | 9

Creating Your Own Plan | 15

Review and Revisions | 15

02   Network Marketing, Solo-Style | 17

Creating a Buzz with Business Cards | 17

Two Cards Double the Odds for Success | 19

Card-Buying Basics | 22

Business Card Follies from the Trenches | 23

Meeting Prospects and Clients Outside of the Office | 26

How to Fit Networking Meetings in Your Schedule | 28

Avoiding Meeting Overload | 29

03   Put It in Print—Direct Mail Marketing Tactics | 31

Words That Make Direct Mail Memorable | 34

Letters | 35

Postcards | 40

Newspaper Subscription Flyers | 46

Surveys | 48

Newsletters | 49

Note Cards | 51

04   Maximum Attention through Print Media Coverage | 53

An Introduction to News Releases | 54

Why News Releases Are Vital to Business | 56

How to Determine What's Newsworthy | 57

Press Release Dos and Don'ts | 59

Getting the Media Involved | 60

Deciding Who Receives Your News | 62

Finding Editors to Receive News | 62

Fifteen Proven Tips for Great Media Relations | 64

Using Editorial Calendars | 66

Online News Release Distribution | 68

05   Making Yourself a Broadcast Media Darling | 73

Why the Broadcast Media Want You | 73

Should You Seek Help to Get Broadcasting Publicity? | 74

A Do-It-Yourself Primer | 74

Satellite Radio | 78

Broadcasts—Live or Taped? | 79

After-Show Follow-up | 81

06   Technological Tools and More That Maximize Marketing | 83

Teleseminars | 84

Directories | 89

Web Videos | 91

Podcasts | 93

Frequently Asked Questions | 95

07 Internet Help to the Rescue | 99

Step 1: Select and Register Your Web Site's Name | 100

Step 2: Research Host Sites | 101

Step 3: Select Web Site Creation Software | 103

Step 4: Review Other Web Sites | 105

Step 5: Create Site Buzz on a Budget | 106

Turning Visitors into Customers | 109

Electronic Newsletters Keep Clients Connected | 109

Creating an Online Press Room | 113

08 Security Issues and Solutions | 117

Security Problems from the Trenches | 117

Physical Security | 119

Intellectual Security: Paranoia Is Healthy | 120

Quick Copyright Tips | 122

Trademarks—Then and Now | 123

Patent Protection | 124

Strategies to Protect Your Property | 124

Backup Options in the Office | 128

Computer Security Strategies | 129

09 Gifts and Other Incentives | 135

How Incentives Increase Business | 136

How Incentives Aid Your Plan | 137

Motivational Events and Ideas | 138

Where to Find Gifts and Incentives | 140

Incentive Products That Increase Loyalty | 145

Incentive Marketing Ideas | 148

10   Six Marketing Ideas for Savvy Soloists | 151

Idea No. 1—Using Accessories to Break the Ice | 151

Idea No. 2—Suitcase Marketing | 153

Idea No. 3—Using Gifts to Produce Results | 155

Idea No. 4—Specialty Regional Web Sites and Publications | 157

Idea No. 5—Preparing for Your Close-up | 159

Idea No. 6—Vehicle Marketing | 161

Time to Put Your Plan to Work | 163

In Summary | 165

Index | 169

Introduction

There you are, changing a baby's diaper or completing a clinical trial on stem cell research, when suddenly a life-changing business idea jumps into your head. The concept borders on brilliant, and it's a perfect product to launch as a solo enterprise maintained at home.

You can see people of all ages, living in different parts of the world, buying and requesting help for extra services needed to successfully use the product. Your bank account grows—first by thousands and then hundreds of thousands—until you reach the one million dollar mark and more.

Life is poised to be a bed of roses. There's just one thing standing between you and success. That obstacle is marketing. It's the hurdle that wasn't addressed in the initial idea.

Marketing, as defined by the American Marketing Association (www.marketingpower.com), is "an organizational function and a set of processes for creating, communicating, and delivering value to customers and for managing customer relationships in ways that benefit the organization and its stakeholders." That's the clinical definition. Marketing means much more to the person who invests his life savings in his own business. Marketing is:

- The unglamorous, behind-the-scenes work performed on a daily basis to make the dream a reality.
- A review of problems and pitfalls associated with why the idea may not launch according to schedule.

- A time-consuming activity that all aspiring business owners should perform but many neglect, which is a common reason why most great ideas follow us to the grave.
- The main ingredient that commits your passion to paper, ensuring long-term success throughout the business life cycle.

Marketing isn't just for large corporations. The speed at which some big firms close shop proves that their marketing failed because it wasn't taken seriously. All the layers of management couldn't devise one workable plan for success.

Things will be different for you. There's just one layer in your organization. You are the person who sets the groundwork and implements the strategy that puts the product or service into the hands of individuals and/or businesses that need it most.

Your marketing campaign starts with this book. Within these covers you will learn the techniques to successfully market in your backyard and around the world twenty-four hours a day, seven days a week.

This book contains many ideas that solo business owners are able to complete on their own. However, no reference source helps if you are not committed to positive action. For example, a plan to contact a television producer to book an appearance is no good without the physical action of picking up the telephone and making the call. If you're ready to be proactive, this is the resource that gets the ball rolling.

What Qualifies Me to Be Your Mentor

Holding court as the featured speaker at one of America's best-known gift shows isn't where I expected my career to go. But here I am, preparing to tell hundreds of attendees how to develop and implement a public relations and marketing strategy.

In 1990 I entered this same show as an attendee, knowing little more about business than could fill a thimble. I remember walking up and down aisles looking at product categories from greeting cards to personal care products. It was a dizzying experience.

Solo Business Statistics

You are not alone in this quest to find and launch a marketing program. According to the 2003 U.S. Census (www.census.gov), 18.6 million independent business owners exist with combined revenues of $830 billion. The word "independent," according to census reports, is defined as a company with no employees.

These are the top-ten independent industries, listed in order of revenue:

1. Real estate, renting and leasing: $176 billion
2. Construction: $126 billion
3. Professional, scientific, and technical services: $103 billion
4. Retail trade: $80 billion
5. General services, too small to separate by category: $65 billion
6. Finance and insurance: $47 billion
7. Health care and social assistance: $46 billion
8. Transportation and warehousing: $45 billion
9. Wholesale trade: $31 billion
10. Administrative support and waste management and remedial services: $28 billion

Don't be concerned if your company's activities fall outside of this list. Many firms in industries large and small, with and without employees, reap the rewards of creating and monitoring marketing strategies that keep their businesses strong and successful.

I stopped to eat at the food court and went to a table where two women sat. We introduced ourselves and traded business cards. The women were based in Virginia and, like me, were starting a business. One of them asked me, "How will you market your business?" I remember mentioning postcard mailings and word-of-mouth promotion, but my game plan was scant. The options were limited for a home-based owner, but I knew better than to give up. How was I to let people know I exist, and how would I position my products as items that attract and benefit individuals and corporations? The question played over and over in my head during the train ride home. When I arrived, the real work started.

Months after attending the show, I consulted library books and newsstand magazines. I attended small business seminars and enrolled in adult school courses. I read success stories about people who started with a little or lots of money. After listing every conceivable way to market, I created a plan using the options at my disposal, steadily adding more ideas until the time was right for implementation.

The work began paying off, and success was steady. Photographs appeared in local newspapers, interviews emerged in business journals and magazines, advertisements played on radio stations, and guest appearances blossomed on television shows. Colleagues around the country saw my name in so many places they asked if I had contracted a publicist. I did; it was me. On that cold train ride home from Washington to New Jersey, knowing that marketing was going to be an uphill battle, I decided to find clients through as many marketing channels as possible. Convincing other people to share my vision was part of the plan. For example, my mother willingly sat in my car, illegally parked between two trucks on New York's Sixth Avenue, while I went into a building to deliver a marketing package to secure an appearance on the Food Network. That's one way a business owner takes chances when the passion for business overwhelms sensibility. I'm not advocating that you break laws, but I am saying that your business life sits squarely in your hands. Sometimes you have to move forward even if you think you'll look out of place or be rejected. That's how a marketing idea works to spread the word about who you are and how your business benefits others.

The last thing I want to do is paint a rosy picture of how everything falls into place when you start marketing. In many cases telephone calls won't be returned. Someone else will get the cover story. Another person will be quoted instead of you, or you'll be misquoted. You'll get upset and maybe shed tears. Some opportunities won't work out, and you'll be glad that others fell apart.

Now it's time for your marketing train to leave the station, destined for opportunities that take you to the top of your industry. Many lessons are about to be learned, and soon you may be just like me, turning your knowledge into a profitable way to put your marketing ideas to good use.

How This Book Is Organized

You hold in your hands the source to dozens of strategies to market products and services. The number of options can literally make you dizzy. My mission is to expose all of the available tools and help you streamline your plan to accomplish the tasks that are manageable by you, a solo business owner. It is important to create an organized marketing campaign that you alone can complete, control, and maintain. That's why this book takes you step-by-step to build your plan.

The first chapter explains all about marketing through the eyes of two business owners. One owns a new firm, and the other mans an ongoing business. Both require marketing support, but the way in which they focus on opportunities is quite different. The sample marketing plans in this chapter illustrate how to integrate separate tasks into one cohesive project and let you see what's possible for your business. A marketing plan will help you focus on your business passion and talent for telling the world your product or service is the next best thing to sliced bread. In addition, the plans introduce you to concepts that we'll discuss in greater detail in the rest of the book.

With this introduction to marketing concepts accomplished, we'll turn our attention to the nuts and bolts of marketing: what's available, how much it costs, problems that may arise, and results that come from completed projects. Chapters 2 and 3 prepare you to spread your business message in professional settings as well as to create and distribute promotional items that convince customers to purchase what you sell.

Getting the media on your publicity bandwagon is the focus of chapters 4 and 5. Whether you seek validation in print or are ready for a televised close-up, these chapters educate you about the process and point you in the right direction.

Home-based business owners cannot prosper without an Internet presence, and that's why chapters 6 and 7 are dedicated to maximizing your reach in cyberspace. When it's time to set up your first Web site, distribute electronic newsletters, create videos, or podcast your message to thousands of listeners, you'll be prepared after reading this tutorial.

After all of your hard work, the last thing you need is to have your competitors take the marketing techniques you create and put their names on it. That's why security issues are discussed in chapter 8. Knowing how to protect your work is especially helpful when creating marketing products that double as intellectual property, a priceless commodity for today's solo business owner.

Chapter 9 helps you decide what types of gifts to buy for loyal customers and where to find these incentive products that keep customers happy and business profitable. This chapter is a must if you appreciate devoted clients and the referral business gained from their word-of-mouth promotion.

The real-life marketing examples throughout this book prove that the phrase "What can happen will happen" is alive and well. Chapter 10 features stories from independent marketers who share challenges and the steps taken to find solutions. At the end, you'll know how to decide which marketing strategies are for you and which are not yet beneficial for your business.

This book contains three types of sidebars.

The ⬎ **Web Watch** sidebar points to URLs (Web addresses) that provide more insight on the adjacent text. It's set up in this manner so that the information is at your fingertips instead of requiring you to consult an appendix.

The **FYI** (For Your Information) sidebar defines terms with which you may not be familiar.

The *Shirley Says* sidebar reveals marketing tips I've experienced that will benefit you.

Caveats to Consider as You Start

As you begin the marketing process, let me share some dos and don'ts to keep in mind.

Do:

- Keep pen and paper by your side as you read this book to jot down ideas at a moment's notice.

- Encourage potential buyers to share their insights about the products and services you sell or plan to sell. Listen to their ideas and incorporate the possibilities. Do not let negative thoughts expressed by others derail your plans (see the list of don'ts for more on this).
- Read news materials to learn how other companies market what they sell and the problems associated with promotion.
- Measure results of your marketing campaigns to understand what works, which areas need more attention, and which should be eliminated.

Don't:

- Allow fear to paralyze you. Mistakes will be made, and each will teach you lessons while moving you closer to smarter marketing decisions.
- Believe that six months of marketing translates into big profits. It will take more time and patience to get your promotional train on track.
- Allow negativity from outside sources to derail your plans. Let your instincts lead you down the path that you believe is best for business.
- Use a buckshot approach when launching plans. In many cases it's wise to test your campaign on a small segment of a larger group. The results help you to fix any problems before distributing the message to a wider audience.
- Attempt to accomplish every marketing idea simultaneously. Choose the ones that make the most sense, incorporating other ideas when the time is right.

When properly performed, marketing ensures that your business gets noticed online and offline by prospects, clients, and the media. It leads to your ultimate goal—sales and more selling opportunities from interested parties who find you through multiple marketing channels.

If you're ready to start, turn the page and let's begin.

01 Your Marketing Plan— The First Step to Success

One of the most difficult processes, outside of the physical work required to put your goals in play, is to create a marketing plan. This chapter introduces you to marketing plan basics.

You may have heard of great plans conceived on napkins, during train rides, or while bathing. All of this is probably true, but where the plan was created isn't important. What is crucial is getting your ideas on paper and into logical order so that you can move from concept to execution.

The marketing plan is a written strategy created by you. It documents how to mold your idea into a full-fledged, revenue-earning business. You may decide to show the plan to trusted advisers who can provide advice and guidance and to investors with money to fund your venture.

Most home-based and small business owners want to leapfrog this process and simply start the business. Neglecting to put your marketing plan on paper, however, is a misstep that has caused chaos and catastrophes for business owners. Some survive, and others promptly go out of business.

If success means anything to you, then it makes sense that the plan to start a business and keep it thriving is worth time and effort. Your long-term success depends on it.

This chapter contains two marketing plans. One focuses on a product-based business, and the other maps the strategy for a service-based firm. Your company will fall into one of these categories, even if you are Web based. Carefully review each firm's goals and objectives. Then refine the ideas to match your own plan.

Marketing Plan No. 1: Product Business

Roger Green owns Teed Up, a golf equipment and sports training firm based in Charlotte, North Carolina. Teed Up helps the general public get acquainted with golf and equips players at every level of experience with tools and support. The company informs customers about the latest products to increase their accuracy and also provides a learning experience to enjoy the game.

Teed Up's golf products are mainly sold online, while services that bring attention and sales to the product line are provided by Roger. The ancillary services that Roger offers help to raise awareness about his products and their availability on request or through the online store.

The company will officially open in six months, and Roger plans to begin marketing the business locally. He hopes to branch out his promotion statewide through a series of sponsorships, targeted mailings, and electronic newsletters.

Roger knows that the golf industry is rife with local suppliers, online competitors, and specialty magazines. He especially understands that his one-man operation will need support on occasion from temporary workers and virtual assistants, but he believes that by marketing within the local area, he can succeed at winning business and gaining loyalty over time. Here's how Roger plans to market.

Teed Up

Charlotte, North Carolina
Roger Green, Owner
Marketing Plan
2007

COMPANY MISSION

MARKET STATISTICS

SPORTS OUTLOOK

MARKETING GOALS

YEAR-1 OBJECTIVES

WEB STRATEGY

GOLF COURSE ALLIANCES

OTHER MARKETING OPTIONS

POTENTIAL PROBLEMS AND SOLUTIONS

YEAR-5 OBJECTIVES

Company Mission

Teed Up focuses on supplying golf equipment, supplies, and support to adults and youth at all skill levels who want the experience to be memorable, successful, and fun.

Market Statistics

Target Market

Adults ages 18–55, youths ages 4–17.

Target Region

Teed Up targets the sixteen counties of the Charlotte metropolitan area.

Regional Statistics

According to the Charlotte Chamber of Commerce's 2006 figures, the region boasts 1.6 million residents, with an annual growth rate of 3.6 percent per year. There is a total of 306,500 households, of which 44.7 percent have a buying income of at least $50,000.

Population by age as of 2005 breaks down as follows:

Age 50 and older—53.9 percent
Ages 35–49—24.5 percent
Ages 25–34—16.9 percent
Ages 18–24—8.8 percent
Age 17 and younger—25.9 percent

Large businesses in the Charlotte area total 894, according to the chamber. The top-five industries are:

Printing—140
Machinery—95
Chemical—64
Furniture—47
Food manufacturing—40

Business information is crucial to my success as Teed Up moves toward partnerships and sponsorships between Year 1 and Year 5.

Sports Outlook

Nongolf Sports

The chamber of commerce brands Charlotte as a "national sports hub." The region plays host to a men's and a women's basketball franchise, a motor speedway, professional football and soccer teams, and minor league baseball and hockey affiliates.

Golf

Charlotte is home to eighty golf courses, two of which are listed in *Golf Digest* as top U.S. courses. The Professional Golf Association's Wachovia championship is played here each May, and other PGA tournaments are located in adjacent states.

Marketing Goals

Year 1

To introduce and sell products and services to 1) area residents who actively participate in sports activities, and 2) independent business owners and company executives who use golf to network and transact business.

Year 5

To build long-term partnerships with local residents, regional businesses, and statewide sports teams, leading to sales from and sponsorships with each segment.

Year-1 Objectives

Adult Market

Golf and other sports are a welcome part of Charlotte's culture. The question here is not how to get adults interested in the sport but rather "How do I create a long-term bond of trust and support to make the name 'Teed Up' synonymous with fun and excitement?" The answer is threefold: benefits, repetition, and nonsports (business and cultural community) memberships and sponsorships.

Benefits. While conducting my own informal surveys, I discovered one central theme echoed by adults who are involved in golfing and those who want to participate: Local golf suppliers do not provide ongoing support to adults who spend thousands of dollars purchasing equipment and supplies.

Along with general marketing to introduce my business and the benefits I provide to clients who enjoy golf during practice and tournament play, I will focus on marketing my postsale support so that adults do not feel abandoned after spending any level of money on tools and equipment. This will be done through postsale contact by phone and e-mail, through mailed postcards with tips, through instructional updates via mailed calendars (also available online once the Web site is established), and through free thirty-minute tutorials for individuals spending $750 or more.

Repetition. A mailing list will be created with names, addresses, and other personal and sports-related information. I plan to mail quarterly postcards and publish a monthly online newsletter to these contacts. The time line will be monitored and changed as needed.

Mailings using these two formats work to keep Teed Up in clients' minds whenever they're ready to learn about new golf products and schedule instructional support. In addition, anyone with school-aged children may see the Teed Up name in school newsletters and on school grounds as we pursue a relationship with the Charlotte educational system.

Nonsports memberships/sponsorships. Introducing and keeping Teed Up's name front and center is part of my goal. That's why it's important to become involved in events that are based on business and social community activities.

This includes memberships and sponsorships at chamber of commerce events, summer concert series, museum galas, and other gatherings that attract individuals and organizations made up of people who golf or have strong potential to make golf part of their lives.

My calendar already includes a list of events that I will attend, from which I will decide which gatherings are worth pursuing for partnerships on a member or sponsorship basis.

Adult Marketing—Custom Services

Teed Up plans to duplicate the same customer service traits as the tie industry by taking golf clubs, shoes, and accessories to businessmen and women within the corporate sector. Offering an "on the road, one-stop shop" at corporate facilities is a convenience that will win many clients.

I have purchased three cases to hold tees, balls, caps, clubs, and other products that golfers frequently request. These cases sit on top of a cart that easily travels in my vehicle and into office buildings. Clients will be able to see what's available in three ways:

1. I will call prospects who are the best targets for selling within offices. Meetings (a better word than "appointments" to use for contact) will be pursued by phone, and I will bring the goods to prospects during business hours.

2. Customers can schedule meetings through a link on my Web site. Once the meeting request is received, I will e-mail a confirmation and confirm again the day before the meeting.

3. Clients can call Teed Up directly to schedule a meeting to see new and frequently used products. Again, I will arrive at their office during business hours to show them requested products and other accessories they may not have considered buying.

This service will be marketed as a time-saver, eliminating the need for clients to drive out of their way to a retail store. Sales are possible not only through the targeted clients but also through associates in the office who golf or want to learn the sport.

Sales through each customized visit are estimated at $300 to $5,000. In addition, information about my Web site, instructional service, youth mentorship program (for their children), and available products and accessories that are not on-site will be discussed before the meeting's conclusion.

Youth Market

Charlotte's educational system, the twenty-third largest district in the United States, contains 150 schools educating 126,903 students in grades pre-K to 12.

Studies have shown that there is a direct correlation between high achievement in school and the discipline students learn through sports participation. Teed Up plans to speak with board of education executives and teachers to introduce a golf training program for students enrolled in grades 4 through 12.

My first step is to research golf programs in school districts throughout the United States to assist me in creating a program for this area (no program exists to date). In addition, I will enlist the help of virtual assistants to call golf centers that have developed these programs to ask questions not answered on their Web sites and to uncover problems associated with program implementation. This will allow me to prepare what-if scenarios that educators will expect me to address.

Finally, this project will begin as a pilot program within three grades—1, 6, and 10—at two of the district's smaller schools. I will test, develop, and refine the project before recruiting outside assistance as Teed Up expands to work with additional grades.

I plan to contact golf product manufacturers to cosponsor the program with supplies for the three pilot grades.

Working with students will help me to accomplish three goals.

1. Secure a lifelong relationship with youngsters as they continue playing golf as adults.

2. Work with parents who, through their children, become enamored with the sport.

3. Brand my company as it becomes aligned with the community and region.

Web Strategy

A Web site URL, host company, shopping cart, and credit card acceptance is in place. The hosting firm's yearly fee is $96, a low fee that allows me to put my marketing dollars to use in other categories.

Teed Up has retained the services of a college intern at a cost of $10 per hour who will create the company Web site. The estimated total cost is $350 for the initial site, after which I will take over the monthly maintenance until one of the virtual assistants working on another project proves to be adept at Web site updates.

The site will contain a mix of information for beginner to advanced players, plus sections for adults and children who have an interest in golf, need to refresh their knowledge after a winter break, or require guidance as they become more proficient.

I visualize the following for the Web site:

Home page. The main page will welcome visitors with images of golfers of various ages and in a variety of settings. Some photos will be pulled from Web site image banks, and others, after obtaining permission, will be images taken of students and me during golf instruction and at events.

Equipment page. Shown on this page is a breakdown of the basic supplies and tools required to play golf. This page will lead to subpages according to age, gender, and skill level. It will also include links to my online shopping cart.

Wardrobe page. Sports-related clothing is an important part of golf. This page will keep visitors informed about fashion trends for all ages and genders as well as provide links to clothing suppliers chosen for their trend-setting styles and Teed Up's ability to partner with them as affiliates.

Frequently asked questions (FAQ) page. Basic questions and answers to general and complex golfing questions are here. This section will be segmented according to topic, such as clubs, etiquette, rules, etc. I anticipate that this area will grow over time and become an important resource to area residents, cementing Teed Up's reputation as a community knowledge bank.

Calendar page. This is a list of instruction schedules and upcoming events planned throughout the Charlotte area in which Teed Up will participate and/or sponsor.

Links page. This area includes Web site links to area golf courses, national magazines, tournament scores, and noncompetitive golf-related sites.

"About us" page. Insights into the company, my golf background, list of clients, and roster of publicity gained through media and print exposure.

Comments page. Clients who provide their insights and experience about our products and services will have their comments posted here. This is also the area where visitors can ask questions about the site. Visitors will be able to include their comments.

Blog. I will dispense a variety of golf tips, promotional photos, and sponsorship events through the blog created to complement my Web site. [*Note:* Blogs are explained in chapter 4.]

Golf Course Alliances

There are many opportunities to work with the area's eighty golf courses, but I plan to start slowly and tactfully to create alliances that do not injure my association with the courses that bring me the most business.

My plan is to work with three courses of varying size that cater to different segments of the Charlotte community. I cannot compete with the on-site pro, nor do I wish to, but I can act as an outside resource when the resident pro is in a position to recommend ancillary services.

Taking selected golf pros to lunch one at a time will put the two of us in a casual setting to discuss the options available for partnerships. During the meal I will ask questions to learn more about:

1. Client characteristics at each facility.

2. Future plans for course upgrades and expansion.

3. Changes that each pro sees occurring locally and in the overall industry.

These answers will help me to understand how to market Teed Up within the region, to golf course management, and to individual adults outside of the facility.

Other Marketing Options

Five more ideas worth pursuing are:

1. Speaking at business and social functions on how golf creates stronger relationships.

2. Creating a printed tip sheet with golf strategies and basic rules of the game.

3. Writing golf articles for submission to Charlotte and North Carolina magazines.

4. Contacting area television and radio shows to learn how to appear on the air to share golf tips with viewers and listeners.

5. Sponsoring youth tournaments and awarding winners with lessons and equipment.

I plan to employ a virtual assistant to help me coordinate this schedule.

Potential Problems and Solutions

Teed Up must be willing and able to make adjustments to this marketing plan if some goals are not achievable. Listed here are areas that may require changes.

Problem: Charlotte's board of education is not agreeable to creating a youth program.
Solution: Work directly with parents who want their children introduced to the sport.

Problem: Meeting with corporate clients at their offices does not net the anticipated sales level per meeting.
Solution: Create an incentive program to encourage additional sales and referral business.

Problem: The Web site's host suddenly ceases business, leaving Teed Up without a Web presence.
Solution: Make sure the Web site is backed up on my own computer. Then search for another, more reliable host and upload my site to its server.

Year-5 Objectives

By 2012 my roots should be firmly planted in Charlotte's golf communities due to the accomplishments achieved in the first five years.
Plans during this stage are to:

1. Assess which activities are bringing the most recognition and sales. Reduce or eliminate lower sales activities.

2. Create a golf school cosponsored by industry manufacturers.

3. Secure a position as a board of director at one of the local golf associations.

These and more plans will be developed and refined as Year 5 approaches.

Marketing Plan No. 2: Service Business

Janet Ross is a certified public accountant (CPA) and owner of AccountAble, an accounting firm based in Denver, Colorado. This is Janet's sixth year in business. Her office is located at home in a den converted into an office. It's a room that has a separate door as an entrance, which makes it easy for clients to visit her if she is unable to go to their home or office.

The start-up phase was busy and profitable as Janet honed her skills at making contact with small and large businesses that became clients. She was able to retain a few jobs from larger CPA firms that recommended her services to small and solo business owners who could not afford the larger companies' fees.

The region's business climate is changing, and Janet knows this by the decreasing size of her clientele. Companies in the area have relocated or consolidated, and the emergence of big box retailers has forced some of Janet's clients to go out of business.

It's a situation that Janet has dreaded, and although she's seen the changes over the past two years, Janet did not take the time to review her marketing plan to decide how to keep her client roster and sales increasing through the change. Janet is experiencing a common hazard of being in business for yourself. You hope that things will stay the same, but they rarely do.

The city's economic development department reports that new companies are considering relocation to the area, but Janet cannot wait for these firms to make their decisions. She needs to revise her marketing plan *now* if she is to survive through regional changes that occur in the future.

One service that Janet has not offered is financial planning. It's a comfortable offshoot to her accounting work that has the potential to bolster and rebrand her firm.

A second service is information sharing through speaking engagements. There are many possibilities for teaming up with banking institutions and city groups, but before Janet pursues this, she must work on her fear of speaking. Although passionate about her work, stage fright has kept her away from the podium. Janet knows that to make potential customers comfortable with her ability, she'll have to get rid of her jitters and start speaking on a regular basis.

A third area for boosting business is adding more printed materials to her roster, materials that are filled with financial planning tips and other ideas that help her clients keep more money in their pockets. Janet knows that out-sourcing firms exist to prepare these important mailing pieces, which she will send to clients at least once per quarter.

Janet wonders why she hadn't considered all of this two years ago, but she won't dwell on the past. It's time to make sure that the sixth and forthcoming years in business are as profitable, if not more so, as the first five. Here's what Janet plans to keep her business thriving.

AccountAble

Denver, Colorado
Janet Green, CPA–Owner
Marketing Plan
2007

COMPANY MISSION—YEAR 1
CURRENT MISSION—YEAR 5
BUSINESS OUTLOOK
CLIENT BASE
MARKETING OPTIONS
WEB SITE ESTABLISHMENT
OTHER OPTIONS
MARKETING TIMETABLE
WRAP UP

Company Mission—Year 1

To provide accounting help to individuals and small business owners who cannot or do not have time to prepare their own income taxes and other tax documents.

Current Mission—Year 5

To 1) provide accounting and financial planning services to high-income individuals, and 2) make my services available to large, local accounting firms that outsource work assigned to them by smaller clients.

Business Outlook

My firm thrived between 2001 and 2004. Sales grew at a rate of 12 percent a year thanks to networking opportunities; work assigned to me by colleagues relocating to other areas; and referrals made by small business clients to colleagues who were starting a business, who were unsatisfied with their accountant, or who decided to focus on their main work rather than keep track of their financials.

The economic climate has changed dramatically in the last two years (only 5 percent growth combined in 2005 and 2006, versus 12 percent from 2001 to 2004). I must now take a look at the big picture to determine how my company will survive as clients decrease due to consolidations, closings, and relocations.

Client Base

My current client roster includes:

1. Four retail businesses (launderette, flower shop, tuxedo rental, and independent party store)

2. Three service businesses (concrete mixer, shoe repair service, and landscaper)

3. Two wholesalers (handbag manufacturer and food broker)

This is approximately half of the business I normally serviced throughout the previous five years. Although business has increased from the remaining firms, there is no guarantee that these companies will stay in business or use my services.

I will continue to provide diligent service to my customers, promoting the new financial services that focus on keeping more money in their pockets.

Other avenues must be pursued to grow my business yet keep within manageable bounds as a solo business proprietor. Considerations are explained within this plan.

Marketing Options

New Opportunity—Speaking Engagements

I envy individuals who can present their topics to audiences small and large. If my business is to stay in the black, I will have to join this enviable group.

The first step is to decide how to translate my industry knowledge into information that the general public understands. Listening to other speakers has taught me that I must balance industry insights with real-life events and humorous stories, all based around accounting. That should not be difficult because of what I've learned and heard from other accountants. The difficult part will be reducing my speaking jitters.

One of my clients, a handbag manufacturer who speaks at trade shows, works with a coach that I will contact for assistance. Her Web site information already has me feeling more at ease. I'm nervous but looking forward to working on this weakness and adding speaking engagements to my list of methods that increase sales.

New Service—Profit Mentoring

Financial planning will be added to my core services. It's an area that I've considered for several years but was too busy to develop. Because I'm aware of clients' tax situations, offering planning help is a natural progression that must be added to assure my firm's longevity.

Word-of-mouth marketing will be used diligently each time I meet with clients at my office or at their location. I can talk about planning strategies in terms of each client's specific situation and how my services will help increase their business and personal growth. Easy-to-understand brochures should be ready to distribute in a few months, which I will carry with me to give to clients after informing them about my additional service. Everyone wants to know how to keep more of the money he or she earns. My pitch will focus on this goal.

New Service—Brochure Distribution

Past methods of distributing information about my firm included a regular-size sheet of paper with my business name at the top and details about my services and rates. Today's clientele expects, and rightfully so, to receive something more professional.

Thank goodness there are companies who specialize in creating brochures and pamphlets for accountants. These firms make general materials available, customized with the accounting firm's name. They also provide mailing services. At the least a brochure keeps clients aware of my service, and at most it can be passed on to associates who read the tips and see my name on the material. This can lead to additional clients or at least to telephone calls or e-mails from prospects.

Two West Coast companies create these customized materials for accounting professionals who don't have time to make their own. After reviewing their Web sites, I will contact them for samples and rates. I'll also contact industry colleagues to learn what type of information they distribute for promotional purposes. Then I will decide which firm is my best option and begin working with them, monitoring the results to see whether or not business stays stable or if added profits occur due to this investment.

Accounting Firm Collaborations

Previous dealings with larger area accounting firms resulted in some work during their peak seasons, which often occurs when my workload is not as stringent. This additional business has blossomed because of relationships created with other accountants at CPA association conferences.

Starting this year I plan to aggressively pursue this type of work. Here are the steps I will take to get more business.

- Call my past contacts to initiate conversations and question my chances to be offered outsourced work in the near future.

- Advertise my accounting specialties in the local chamber of commerce publication and state accounting magazine. This strategy will cost $125 and $150 per year, respectively, for a four-inch ad.

- Pursue a feature story in the local newspaper on how small businesses serve the needs of larger firms. The feature-story editor and I are members of the same women's group. She may be interested in this type of article, which will serve to promote my services to firms that read the article.

The opportunity to work with larger accounting firms may be closed because of internal consolidations, but such consolidation might make this a viable option because of fewer accountants on their payrolls. In either case, making more accounting firms aware of my presence and abilities will open the door to new relationships.

Web Site Establishment

My main focus has been on building and maintaining a solid roster of clients who use my accounting services throughout the year. The Internet was not part of my planning, but adding a Web site to market my services has the potential to help me to secure new clients.

The office is equipped with Internet capabilities. Outside of that, I have not considered a Web site name, software to create a site, or any of the other components necessary to market in this manner.

At a recent networking meeting, I spoke with a woman who is a trusted resource on Internet practices. She provided me with several educational Web site addresses and her own manual, all which explain the details associated with starting and maintaining a Web site.

This expert agreed to help me establish a site, including selecting a name and host. I will provide her with information for site creation. The initial material, developed after reviewing accounting-based Web sites in other states, includes:

1. Basic information about my firm and the types of businesses that use my service

2. A roster of current and former clients

3. A list of IRS calendar schedules and timetables for tax completion

4. Year-round tips to help visitors prepare for tax time

5. A page explaining why individuals and businesses should hire me to keep them financially on track, and various options to contact me

This Web site and all the necessities to get it up and running will cost approximately $2,000 and has the potential to bring me additional business in the long run. It will certainly help clients and prospects become aware of my services, whether they are currently in town or moving to this area.

OTHER OPTIONS

Self-imposed brainstorming sessions conducted in the past two weeks have developed the following ideas for further consideration:

1. Donate no more than three accounting consultations at the next black-tie charity.

2. Purchase customized travel logs for distribution to customers who use their own cars for business.

3. Create an association of service professionals who learn from each other and recommend each other's services to their respective clients.

4. Conduct a specialized accounting/financial class through a local adult school for product and service-based business owners.

5. Distribute an online newsletter when my Web site is operational.

Marketing Timetable
Public Speaking Support

- Make contact with speaking coach: this month (March).

- Work with coach to reduce speaking anxiety: three months (May to July).

- Create a roster of three accounting-related seminars of forty-five minutes each: two months (June and July).

- Call a maximum of six groups to book speaking engagements: throughout March. (Calls must be made early in the year due to each group's booking schedules.)

- Secure first speaking opportunity: between October 2007 and January 2008.

Profit Mentoring

- Decide on the specialty financial areas I will offer (SEP retirement funds, employee profit sharing, etc.): first quarter.

- Review clients' files to determine services each needs most: first quarter.

- Alert clients to new mentoring program: ongoing through the year.

- Create brochures with mentoring information: first or second quarter (see "Brochure Distribution"). If the brochures are ready within the second quarter, they can be distributed to prospects and clients as a follow-up to conversations we've had regarding profit mentoring.

Brochure Distribution

- Request brochure samples from printers: first quarter.

- Speak with colleagues regarding their distribution sources: January and February.

- Determine which brochures are best for marketing purposes: first quarter.

- Order brochures: second quarter.

- Determine which brochures look best to raise business awareness: ongoing.

Note: Brochure order should be timed with securing Web site and e-mail addresses (see info under "Web Site Establishment").

Accounting Firm Collaborations

- Contact firms that have provided me with past work: ongoing.

- Contact colleagues at additional firms whom I have met at industry meetings and other gatherings: January and February and from May onward.

- Determine which opportunities are likely and pursue potential business and collaborative work: ongoing; review each month.

- Secure advertising with trade magazines and the chamber of commerce newspaper to market subcontracting experience: ASAP at yearly rate.

Media Promotion

- Contact feature-story editor with article idea: January, March, ongoing.

- Stay in touch with editor for other article ideas through her or news colleagues: ongoing.

Web Site Establishment

- Review accounting-based Web sites to determine and finalize my site's details: first quarter.

- Set up appointment to meet with Web site consultant and finalize project: first or second quarter.

- Determine when Web site name and host will be obtained: first quarter.

- Order new stationery and business cards that include Web site information: second quarter.

- Ensure that Web site and e-mail information are added to brochures: see "Brochure Distribution" above.

Other Options

- Review brainstorming ideas on a quarterly basis. Work on ideas that are ready for launch, add projects for consideration, and eliminate ideas that no longer fit within the marketing plan.

Wrap Up

The sooner my plan is put into action, the better. Therefore, most of my goals will begin immediately and be completed by midyear. Timing plays a big part in this plan because of 1) the accounting period from January to April, 2) my need to secure my client roster, and 3) the desire to create marketing materials and increase my client list.

Many of my plans focus around making telephone calls or requesting information by e-mail. I can review and approve requested materials before the workday begins and in the evening.

Creating Your Own Plan

Each of the two marketing plans we've examined has room to address additional details and ideas. Both provide the essential parts of a well-designed strategy. Your plan's elements depend on numerous factors, many of which are addressed by Teed Up and AccountAble. A well-rounded marketing plan includes:

Mission statement: The defining sentence that explains your business's focus.

Business overview: An honest look at what you plan to sell and why it's beneficial to the target market.

Target market: Facts related to potential buyers, including their characteristics, geographic location, and other supporting documentation.

Marketing goals: A list of actions that outlines how the plan will connect products and services with customers. This encompasses every opportunity in print, by word of mouth, through broadcast channels, and on the Internet.

Marketing objectives: A breakdown of steps to accomplish each goal.

Other goals for consideration: A list of additional marketing options. These are ideas that did not make the short list but could be considered for implementation in the future.

Financial aspects: A monetary breakdown of costs associated with each goal. Costs can be separated throughout the financial subsection or integrated within the goals' structure.

Timetable: A recap of all goals and objectives, matched with an overview of when each is scheduled for completion.

Plan B: No plan is foolproof, which means that some problem is almost guaranteed. List the likely problems and solutions to put in place at a moment's notice. A plan B strategy appears in the Teed Up marketing plan.

Review and Revisions

Create your own timetable to keep the marketing plan up to date and on schedule. A monthly review is recommended, but only you know what works for your business. Post a reminder system on your wall or desk calendar or in your electronic calendar.

Stay on schedule. Your efforts will pay off, and marketing will become as habitual as waking each morning.

If you stop consulting the plan for a period of time, don't discard it completely. The best marketers occasionally get sidetracked. Pick up the plan, review it, make updates, and get your business back on track. As long as you're still in business, it's not too late to try again.

Network Marketing, Solo-Style

The act of networking is often discussed in newspaper and magazine articles, in which experts share networking tips or advice on how not to network. What all home-based business owners want to know is 1) what's the best way to promote my business to new acquaintances, and 2) what types of events can I attend to meet like-minded people? Both questions are answered in this chapter. At the end you'll feel confident and ready to start conversations that blossom into profitable opportunities.

Creating a Buzz with Business Cards

When you find yourself on an airplane 38,000 miles above the earth, that position tends to secure a captive audience willing to hear your message and exchange ideas. It's also a place to have plenty of business cards ready for distribution.

While traveling I use a Palm Pilot and wireless keyboard rather than a laptop to type letters and check my schedule. People are genuinely mesmerized by technological products not seen every day, and thus the Palm and keyboard are my tools to create networking situations quicker than any laptop on the market. Getting attention from passengers and flight attendants without saying a word is the best way to make friends on a flight. Once the Palm and keyboard are in place on the tray table, all eyes focus on me, and that's when I know I'll be passing out lots of business cards.

One passenger always breaks the silence, and the questions begin. "What's that?" "What does it do?" "How does it work?" I introduce the onlooker to the product, then I explain who I am and what I do as well as find out about the people around me. From there, business cards are exchanged across the aisle. Passengers who don't carry cards participate by writing their names and telephone numbers on paper. They don't dare be left out of this flying party.

That's one way to hold court and build relationships. This book will reveal many more.

The business card is your personal billboard, reminding contacts who you are, what you do, and how your products and services benefit them, their companies, and personal lives. Success in business depends on your ability to put business cards in the hands of everyone you meet, wherever the gathering occurs. You'll be shaking lots of hands to get your business name in places where buyers exist, including business meetings, baseball games, and bonfires. And that means handing out business cards during the conversation. It doesn't matter whether cards are exchanged at the introduction or conclusion, just so long as you make sure to complete the social period by handing out a permanent reminder.

FYI: Business card information. www.solobusiness marketing.com/basics/businesscards.htm

Business cards wield lots of power. They are also incredibly inexpensive, especially when you

consider the part that distribution plays to increase your profitability. Most cards include basic information to ensure that prospects and clients can contact you in a manner that matches their lifestyles:

- Your name
- Title or occupation
- Business name
- Business slogan
- Address (street or post office box)
- City, state, zip code
- Telephone number
- Fax number
- Web site address
- E-mail address

Shirley Says

Street Address or P.O. Box?

Blogs and message-board discussions on the Internet weigh the pros and cons of using a street address versus a post office box number on a business card when your office is located at home. What truly matters is your image, expertise, and professionalism at meetings and social gatherings. As long as you present yourself properly, no one will care about or question your address.

That list of business card necessities seems too extensive to include on thick, coated pieces of paper approximately two-by-three-and-one-half inches in size, but it fits as shown in the examples on page 20. You can elect to put everything on your card or exclude what's not needed.

Details such as fax number and e-mail address are omitted by some business owners because of spam they receive as a result of distribution. They release those two items on an as-needed basis.

It's surprising to find that some new business owners overlook the basics when creating their first card. I receive business cards without area codes, cards without a person's name, and cards that exclude the city and state. These omissions occur because the cards' owners expect to distribute their message only in local settings. But why not include all the information, especially since there's no extra printing charge to do so?

Graphics are another issue. You want your business card to be memorable, but not because of something disjointed, such as a symbol on the card that doesn't match your business type. If you don't have a logo, or if there is no symbol for your industry, a card without graphics is acceptable.

FYI: Logo definition. www.mda.mo.gov/AgBusiness/ resources/business_logo.htm

Three more no-no's are misspellings, crossed-out words, and penned-in words. Business cards are too important for your image to appear messy. Double-check each and every line of your card before placing an order. Use a magnifying glass, eyeglasses, or reading glasses to inspect every character. If your address or phone number changes, order new cards immediately. The price is quite affordable, and gaining new business through card distribution is worth the expense.

Here are other details you'll want included on your business cards, depending on each item's importance to connect with customers.

- Cell phone number
- Computer instant messaging identification/screen name
- Telephone numbers for additional locations
- Voice mail number
- Your photograph (a tactic used frequently by real estate agents)
- Shipping address (if not the same as the main address on the card)
- State-issued business license number (Service professionals add this to establish credibility.)
- Hours of operation
- Location directions

Two Cards Double the Odds for Success

Many solo and home-based business owners cater to more than one industry. If this is true in your business, having two cards rather than one is a smart investment. For example, you may work with retailers and wholesalers within the same industry. Distributing one business card to both groups may not allow you to convey the right message in each case. Carrying two distinct cards works to your advantage. (See my two business cards on the next page.)

There's no need to change your business name when creating two cards, unless that's part of your strategy, but your slogan or phone number may vary. One group might receive a card with a plain, white background, while the

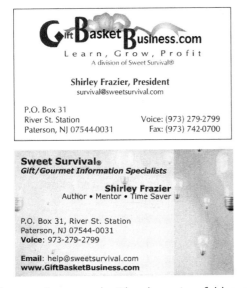

other receives a card with color or in a fold-over configuration. This difference helps you easily distinguish between cards and thus present the correct one to a prospect.

To make matters more complex, there are more formats on the market than the traditional matte or glossy coating. Here's a short list of features business card suppliers offer.

Metallics. Silver, gold, or platinum is forged into a business card that's indestructible except when inserted into a shredder. This configuration is for entrepreneurs who believe a metallic card is required because of their industry status or because of the level of achievement they wish to convey. Keep this option in mind for upgrading purposes, not for creating your first card. Your money is better spent elsewhere.

Wood grain. Your name and all particulars are etched into a card that simulates wood. High-end construction companies may opt for this, and it's

popular with companies that catch, sell, or distribute fish products.

Rounded edges. Business card makers are cutting corners, literally, smoothing 90-degree edges into rounded ends. The look is considered by some as a step up from traditional cards without being over the top. Women may prefer this style more than men.

Confections. Business cards made from chocolate pressed into molds have been around for years, created and distributed only when making an impression counts. The basic paper card is usually included along with the chocolate version in case the recipient eats the confection, leaving nothing but a sweet memory of your initial meeting.

You're charged with starting and completing so many marketing details that you can't possibly remember everything to include on your business cards. The Business Card Checklist in

Shirley Says

Busting Business Card Myths

Many new entrepreneurs believe that their business cards should be distributed sparingly. This myth is far from true. Smart business owners know that their cards are to be distributed as fast as humanly possible. Another myth is that you should exchange business cards only with qualified prospects and leads. Not so! Any person who possesses your card, no matter what his or her industry, has the ability to share that card with another person who may be waiting to conduct business with you.

Business Card Checklist

Primary Details	Write Your Input Here	Check Here to Omit on Card
Your Name		❏
Your Title		❏
Business Name		❏
Business Slogan		❏
Business Address		❏
Room, Floor, Suite		❏
City, State	_____ , _____	❏
Zip Code		❏
Telephone Number (include area code)	( )	❏
Fax Number (include area code)	( )	❏
Web Site Address	www. _____ . ____	❏
E-mail Address	_____ @ _____ . ____	❏

Optional Details

Cell Phone Number	( )	❏
Additional Location(s) (Street/City/State/Zip)		❏
Shipping Address (Street/City/State/Zip)		❏
Voice Mail Number/Pager	( )	❏
Internet Screen Name		❏
Photograph		❏
Professional License Number		❏
Hours of Operation		❏
Location Directions		❏

this chapter will help you pinpoint every detail to include on your cards before placing an order. When the cards arrive, remember to check them for accuracy and to distribute them briskly. You deserve to tell everyone you meet who you are, what you do, and how you benefit them personally and professionally.

Card-Buying Basics

Commercial printers and business mail-order catalogs were once the only sources of buying business cards. Today the Internet dazzles us with new methods of putting the perfect message onto cards of any shape, quantity, and color. You may already have a stack of business cards on hand, but don't let familiarity with one printer stop you from discovering what's available through other sources.

As you evaluate potential suppliers, look for the one who meets your criteria. Your card's appearance is a major consideration, and so is price, which varies between local and online suppliers. You will want a company that will create cards to you specifications and that will have them ready for pickup or delivery in a timely manner. But there's one more ingredient that completes this recipe: service. Service makes the difference between selecting one business card supplier over another. Once you find a supplier that meets these criteria, order your traveling billboards and be ready to distribute them wherever you travel.

Here's a look at the types of suppliers you can consider to create your business cards.

Commercial Printers

These local superstars compete heavily against online competitors. Local suppliers make themselves known through neighborhood business groups, trade magazines, and charitable events. Their prices may not be as low as other suppliers, but the cost is still affordable. There are pluses: Working with local commercial printers keeps the region's economy thriving, and a relationship with this source can create numerous business opportunities that cannot be secured through online vendors.

Office Supply Stores

These retailers capitalize on location to offer more than the usual workplace products. While picking up toner, paper, and clips, you can browse through a large binder filled with business card styles and logos ready to order on the spot. Making a purchase is easy, and cards can be picked up usually within two weeks of the order date. As with any print order, you must make sure that no part of the card layout is overlooked. One disappointing experience may cause you to seek another supplier in the future.

➤ Staples: www.staples.com. Office Depot: www.officedepot.com. Office Max: www.officemax.com.

Web-Based Business Card Suppliers

Online templates that make business card creation simple and easy command a business owner's attention. That's why Internet card suppliers enjoy growing popularity. Competition between card suppliers has dropped prices to new lows. But low cost does not always amount to a quality card, as some online purchasers assert from experience.

Ordering online means you must familiarize yourself with product terminology—"matte," "glossy," "100-pound paper," among other technical specifications. Business owners and others who've purchased business cards online give both glowing accounts and scathing reports about their experiences. Take these findings with a grain of salt as you perform your own research, which includes asking people within your industry and circle of friends which online suppliers deliver quality cards and great service.

Software

FYI: Business card templates. Avery: www.avery.com (click the "Cards" link).

Business card software, used in conjunction with your computer and printer, is another option that business owners choose for several reasons.

1. Cards ordered from an outside source won't arrive in time for an upcoming event, so temporary cards are created in-house.

2. Creative individuals thrive on the challenge of designing their own cards. When finished, a copy is delivered to an outside printer to reproduce it in exact specifications. Reproduction isn't always possible, but determined business owners find a way to make their design a reality.

3. Certain situations, such as the immediate need to promote a new product or service, call for altered cards. When there's no time to order through traditional channels, printing temporary cards on perforated business card paper, purchased at an office supply store, is a quick solution.

Business Card Follies from the Trenches

Exchanging business cards should be an easy and forthright process. You hand one person your card as she reciprocates with her own. But you wouldn't believe how unnecessarily complicated business card distribution can get! Here are situations I've faced that show what not to do when exchanging cards.

The Cosmetic Kamikaze

Coming home from a speaking engagement makes me happy for two reasons. First, the time spent away from the office meeting people and sharing business tips is incredibly satisfying. Second, I'm going back to my base to develop ideas I've collected. This double scoop of joy puts me off guard when I'm at the airport waiting to board the plane.

A woman approached me, placed her business card on the chair's armrest, and announced she'd be right back. I took one look at the card and saw her affiliation with a cosmetics firm. There was no doubt that a sales pitch was about to begin. She'd probably offer a bonus: the opportunity for me to sell the same cosmetics under her guidance.

My premonition was right. She returned, barely said "hello," and began to unload information on all the benefits I would receive by selling cosmetics. Do you see the problem? There was no formal introduction, no questions about why either of us is in town or about our personal expertise. She saw me as an opportunity rather than as a person with whom to build a business relationship.

This woman attempted to sabotage my peace, so I interrupted her and announced that I had no interest in selling the products she represents. She didn't listen and started her pitch a second time. That's when I said, "Have a good day," and began reading a book taken from my briefcase.

Attempts to force-feed a new contact with your mode of thinking is not the way to make a business card connection. But it is good training in one aspect: This approach shows you how some people treat others under the guise of networking and warns you not to make the same mistake.

Not all people in the cosmetics industry practice bully tactics, but I've met my share. Some people want you to make a detour from your plans and join them. There's nothing wrong with adding another dimension to your business if it works as part of the total package. But apples and oranges don't mix. If your business consists of owning and operating vending machines, and that's where you want to spend your time and energy, another person's encouragement to sell a product that takes you away from your core business delays your success. Wish the other person well, and stay on track. Continue searching for individuals who appreciate and respect the true reason for exchanging business cards.

The "Not Getting to Know You" Method

While waiting for a speaker to begin his seminar at a New York conference, I sat in a room with other attendees and started conversations to discuss their backgrounds and uncover ideas on how we might do business together. It was a standing-room-only crowd, and everyone spoke in muffled tones as they waited for the seminar to start.

Another attendee walked to the front of the room and began distributing her business card to each of us. She wasn't the speaker; she simply started giving out her cards without saying a word. Some people refused to take the card. Others asked her why she was doing this, and she responded, "I'm just trying to network." Her networking plan was a disaster, and you can understand why. Business cards don't cost much, but they're not meant to be wasted. Not only was this an exercise in futility, but she also harmed her reputation and image.

Networking is about making connections, finding common ground, and sharing information that propels the success of both parties. Blind exercises such as this create no allies or business opportunities.

After hearing the speaker and making final connections, I walked out of the room and noticed the misguided networker's business cards left behind on seats and the floor. Hopefully she learned better networking techniques before her business dreams disintegrated.

Wasting Another Person's Time and Money

Trade shows are events where I conduct seminars. I also connect with exhibitors, reinvigorating old relationships and learning about new products. But there was a time when I was on the other side of the exhibit table, showing my products and trying new tactics to convince people to buy.

I must have participated in at least fifty trade shows, and at each one there were plenty of people soliciting *me* for business. Rather than invest in a booth to market their products, these impolite solicitors attempted to take away the time and money I invested in renting a booth to sell me on their products and services. Anyone who has rented an exhibit space knows these tactics well. As a novice exhibitor I was open to this approach at my first event, but during the show some solicitors were upset that I didn't spend as much time with them as I did with customers who were

making purchases. By show's end I had a heavy box full of marketing materials from these solicitors, which I left behind for garbage collection.

The next event was handled differently. When a solicitor approached my booth, I gave him my business card and told him that if he wanted my full attention, he'd use my card's address to mail the package to me. Serious businesspeople who want to build their businesses will send the information to you by mail, along with a proper letter of introduction. If not, nothing's lost on your end.

This type of situation illustrates why printing separate business cards is a wise investment. If you are a trade show exhibitor, distribute one card to legitimate prospects and hand the other card to everyone else.

"Take My Card, but I Don't Want Yours"

Networking at luncheons is tricky. You can never be sure who will be dining at the same table. There will be times when you're fortunate enough to be surrounded by like-minded people and other times when it seems no one has anything in common with you. But something different happened to me in Texas.

"Hi, I'm Diane Davis," said the woman next to me. I introduced myself and did the same with others seated at the table. As the afternoon progressed we exchanged business stories and listened to the speakers. The event ended, and I offered my card to Diane. She reached for her card and said in a matter-of-fact tone, "I won't take your card, but I want you to take mine."

I felt a puzzled look cover my face. Where did Diane learn to network, and how did this one-way card exchange benefit her with people she'd met in the past? I was too stunned to ask and left her business card on the table. Why would I contact such a person?

Exchanging business cards is exactly how it sounds. It is an exchange so that individuals who have made each other's acquaintance can contact one another in the future. Take the other person's card. If you do not want it, discard it after the event, or throw it away in your office.

Insulting a person by declining her card will make you no friends, and you'll need lots of friends to grow your business. They'll not only help you but also be a source of support for others within your circle. The wider your circle, the more powerful your influence in your industry and others.

Meeting Prospects and Clients Outside of the Office

Home is where many solo business owners make their money, working in a designated room with a computer, printer, and fax machine. Home is also the place where babies cry, dogs bark, and dust bunnies gather when a broom isn't within reach. There's no way we want our clients and allies meeting us here. That's why we need to get out into the world and make connections in open environments where others gather for the same purpose.

Remember the army poster with the picture of Uncle Sam pointing outward and stating, "I Want You!"? That's the same way hotels, coffeehouses, and bookstores feel about your presence in their facilities. They welcome your planned and impromptu meetings. They realize the profit potential from the small and solo business sector and, in the true spirit of marketing, will do anything to win your dollars.

Retailers and service organizations want us to come to them for informal meetings for several reasons.

1. They look busy. If lots of people are meeting informally, coming in and out at a steady pace, their location looks like a hub of excitement, the in place to be. Business owners prefer this type of setting, one with an energetic environment and tolerable noise level. Word spreads when a facility gains this reputation, and popularity is key to everyone's business success.

2. They sell products. Meetings tend to include sharing a meal or beverage. In the course of sixty minutes, one table has the potential to host three twenty-minute meetings. Such turnover keeps the register ringing all day long. This win-win situation allows the facility to maintain profitability while home-based owners make connections.

3. They become familiar, and so do you. Recognizable faces get perks, such as better

seating and other incentives that infrequent visitors won't get. This bonding tactic benefits both parties. You can't predict how a first-time meeting will fare, but your surroundings in this comfort zone will keep you focused and on track.

By catering to your need to meet outside of the home office, these facilities are happy to make cozy spaces available within their shops. They understand that the more comfortable you feel holding meetings at these well-lit and secure places—which in rural and suburban settings have plenty of parking as a bonus—the more likely you will be to plan larger gatherings at that location and order meals or desserts. More individuals are joining the business start-up bandwagon, which means more service-based companies will be searching for ways to cater to you.

Before you book a meeting, choose a day to visit the places in your area that are prime candidates for a get-together. Weekend visits are no good. You want to experience each setting at the time you'll visit, and the odds are that you be there sometime between Monday and Friday. Here are key features to check.

Configuration. Does the place have adequate seating during the time of your visit? Is a separate meeting room available in case you wish to speak privately with your guests?

Crowd. Are long lines of customers waiting for service because a skeleton crew is working at that time, or is the staff-to-customer ratio adequate to accommodate steady business as it arrives?

Cleanliness. How does the staff maintain the facility as customers move from the front door to the order counter to the seating area and back through the front door? Do napkins, stirrers, and spilled beverages litter the floor, waiting for a customer to be injured? How quickly do staff members address cleanliness, or do they walk with their heads tilted upward in an attempt to ignore hazards? Are tables dirty and sticky as though a group of third graders visited minutes before you entered?

Comfort. Does the facility seem to mind your visit if you work at a table without buying food or beverage? You'll know the answer if the staff watches your movement or informs you of a nonposted rule that says you must buy if you intend to stay.

Convenience. How far is the facility from your office? Is there lots of traffic in the area or noise inside the shop due to car horns or truck transportation? Reviewing each potential meeting place lets you know which one is easiest to reach, but a fast commute means little if the other key attributes don't add up.

Your search may uncover other meeting nooks in your community, such as private library rooms, teahouses, and restaurants with designated meeting spaces. The latter two will generally expect you to order food and drinks, but there will be plenty of times when you wish to share a meal with prospects and business allies.

The bottom line is this: Your business lifestyle makes you a hot commodity to facilities that recognize the profit potential of having you and others like you patronize their spaces. The number of home-based business owners is growing at a rapid pace. More meeting places are being planned right now by smart shops, restaurants, and others who want a piece of the action.

How to Fit Networking Meetings in Your Schedule

One thing that busy solo and home-based business owners have in common is time constraints. There are so many projects to manage and many more opportunities waiting for attention that it may seem difficult to fit networking into your schedule. That's what I used to think. Because everything rides on our shoulders, making time for networking puts our ability to make money in jeopardy. Or does it?

Meeting people at events and using business cards to confirm connections are activities that guarantee a healthy, thriving enterprise. Sitting at a computer all day long does not. That said, the computer is a tool to make online connections, as we'll discuss in chapter 6. It's also one place where networking functions are found. Here are places to look.

FYI: Business newspapers. Crain's: www.crains.com. **Technology Web sites.** Microsoft: www.microsoft.com. Adobe: www.adobe.com. Hewlett-Packard: www.hp .com.

- Business newspapers
- Technology Web sites that conduct nation-wide seminars
- Business communities
- Local and national business groups

Make it a habit to review the local newspapers. Business meeting news is usually printed on Monday, but your paper's schedule may differ. Most newspapers have an online component, so if you don't subscribe to the print version, check the newspaper's Web site for a meeting calendar.

Networking meetings are different than conferences, which are all-day and multiday gatherings focused on a certain business or industry. The most popular meeting types are as follows.

Mixers

Expect a two- to three-hour event where people in business get together, usually on a Wednesday or Thursday evening, to relax and speak with as many people as possible within the event's time frame. Lots of people are meeting for the first time, and others are getting reacquainted with old friends and allies. Mixers have a tendency to be ear-challenging events. Lots of people are talking at once, which makes for a decibel-elevating experience.

Business over Breakfast

These gatherings are attended by business owners who are too busy during the day for luncheons but need to get out of the office to refresh their focus. Breakfast usually consists of bagels, muffins, coffee, and tea. The cost is nominal, especially in relation to the people you meet and the interaction that occurs in this sixty- to ninety-minute gathering. I favor this type of meeting because it gets you up and out in the morning when most business owners are fresh, idea inspired, and ready to interact with others in a casual setting. It jumpstarts your day with a mix of networking and business trends to consider until the next breakfast meeting.

Lunch and Learn

If you're looking for a networking event that is two hours or less, where meeting other business owners and enjoying a meal is combined with hearing a speaker, then luncheons are for you. The gathering is structured and fast paced to make the most of your time and get you back to the office for a productive afternoon. This is a terrific midday event for those who enjoy a break in their workday. It's also the preferred choice for people who cannot attend evening events because of family obligations.

Dinner and Dialogue

Dinner meetings feature a speaker who shares ideas to expand your business horizons. This gathering is more expensive than the other get-togethers mentioned here, but not so much that it's unaffordable. Many business owners prefer to end their day by comparing notes with others and learning smarter ways to organize and

streamline their workload. For home-based owners who cannot otherwise get out of the office, attending at least one dinner meeting a month is a worthwhile investment.

You'll find other business gatherings in your area sponsored by the chamber of commerce, local clubs, industry-specific groups, and national associations. Groups that host these events understand that there is strength in numbers, so expect to be asked to consider joining a group whenever you attend a function.

Avoiding Meeting Overload

Attending too many meetings in one week may cause you to become meeting weary and postpone signing up for upcoming sessions. To make sure this doesn't occur, decide which events are best at this particular moment in business. Every meeting will not be for you; choose the ones that match your current needs. Your selections may hinge on:

- Industries that bring together the most qualified leads.
- Time of day that's best for you to attend.
- Types of meeting you prefer (industry specific, meal and speaker, etc.).

Are you the type of person who doesn't like going to meetings because it's difficult to interact with others, yet you realize that such interaction is critical to your success? Then you're in luck. Every meeting is filled with outgoing individuals who are happy to introduce you to others. You'll feel more comfortable making your way through crowds of people with help from a group's ambassador rather than getting through it on your own. Call the event number and request such a person to guide you on arrival.

Be aware that shyness can work to your advantage, because your listening skills take control. Many people don't listen to others; they simply wait their turn to talk. You, however, will be ready to concentrate on each word spoken by the person in front of you, and that's the best way to learn and grow.

Seasoned business owners consider themselves pros when it comes to exchanging business cards and networking with customers and allies, but we all need a refresher course from time to time. That's what this chapter provides, a new and renewed approach to guarantee lifelong connections.

03

Put It in Print—
Direct Mail Marketing Tactics

This chapter examines reasons why an investment in direct mail is important to your marketing campaign. Letters, brochures, surveys, and more are addressed in this chapter, as well as how to introduce and close the deal by mail and alternatives to doing everything on your own. Best of all, you'll realize that direct mail is affordable. You just have to learn where to find the goods that tell the world you're the best in the industry. Let's get started.

"Thank goodness for the Internet." That's the sentiment of home-based business owners worldwide whose eyes opened to a new way of reaching and selling to customers. No more counting solely on telephone calls and direct mail correspondence to reach individuals and businesses with words that convince them to buy. Yes, the Internet is excellent. The Web put solo businesses on the map with twenty-four-hour-a-day storefronts. However, the Web will never eclipse the need to market with direct mail, the process of connecting with clients through postal mail using letters, postcards, note cards, and other printed materials. Electronic and printed marketing work hand in hand to capture customer attention and make believers out of prospects who decide that what we have works for them.

Why can't we use the Web as our main marketing method and skip direct mail altogether? A report issued in September 2004 by the National Telecommunications and Information Administration provides clear reasons why business owners cannot depend solely on the Internet to reach prospects.

- Percentage of U.S. population with no Internet access from any location: 41.3 percent
- Percentage of U.S. households with no Internet access: 32.4 percent
- Reasons given for non-Internet use:
  - Don't need/not interested—41.6 percent
  - Too expensive—22.9 percent
  - No or inadequate computer available—22.5 percent

These statistics lead to one conclusion: There is still a significant number of people without Internet access. These people have no access to your Web site, so they call or write asking for information. My potential buyers often write or call me to ask for a catalog and other printed literature. I used to tell each caller to visit the Web site, but many said they did not have easy access. That told me I was neglecting non-Internet buyers. This is why direct mail is and will always be an important part of the marketing puzzle, connecting us with people who want what we sell.

National Telecommunications and Information Administration: www.ntia.doc.gov/reports/anol/NationOnlineBroadband04.htm

There's another reason why your marketing must include printed products. People with Internet access often want details by mail. They desire something in their hands that tells them more about your product or service.

To some, information sent by direct mail is

Shirley Says

Electronic or Print? Look to Your Market

Generation Xers (people born in the 1960s and 1970s) and Generation Yers (people born in the 1980s and 1990s) are big Internet users. They think differently from members of the baby boom generation, who did not grow up with computers in their homes and offices. Middle-aged and older adults respect printed materials. To them, a letter, brochure, or catalog gives an item more credibility. It's an art form that makes a product or service come alive with a mix of text and photographs. If you cater solely to customers age fourteen and under, perhaps the Internet is all you need. But if your target market is adults, creating direct mail products is a wise investment. The Web cannot be your only marketing tool if you are to succeed in the long run.

seen as more credible than an item sold exclusively on the Web. After all, anyone can create a Web site. There's so much on the Internet that's fraudulent compared to what's sold through printed mail, especially since business owners invest time and money to produce and ship a letter, brochure, catalog, or flyer through the mail. "Surely it's a worthy product if the business owner took the time to craft paper into a sales piece," some folks think.

This is what customers say to themselves. They want to hold a piece of paper in their hands, something that convinces them that your product saves time or lightens their load. When you visit a professional office—such as that of a doctor, dentist, or accountant—literature about their services is spread around the waiting room.

Brochures and newsletters act as informational pieces, and each includes a Web site address where more details are found. These professionals understand that a Web site is another tool that helps them win clients. This is the same way to view your site.

What if there were no Internet? You'd be forced to create direct marketing pieces, send news releases regularly to media personnel, attend trade shows where your products and services would be shown, make television appearances, and solicit magazine quotes and advertisements. Even in the age of the Internet, none of these opportunities can be overlooked. All should be completed regularly as part of your marketing strategy, and all lead to sending direct mail to prospects who will migrate to your Web site for a closer look before buying, subscribing, or calling.

E-mail works as another tool in your marketing arsenal, providing customers with information about you in another format. Web sites and e-mail both work effectively with direct mail, the more-expensive part of the trio due to the cost of printing and mailing literature to prospective customers.

Creating direct mail products was once incredibly expensive. In the past these products were available only through commercial printers, some of whom lacked the capacity to print graphics that add credibility to mailed literature. But thanks to modern technology, you can create direct mail pieces for a fraction of what it used to

Shirley Says

E-mail as a Marketing Tool

Using e-mail as your exclusive client connection source, rather than combining it with direct mail contact, is quickly becoming a marketing obstacle. E-mail is a cost-effective way to reach customers because of the low-to-no cost factors, but spammers have made e-mail a liability rather than a resource.

According to ClickZ Network, e-mail contact continues to drop in popularity because of spam-related mail and because filters installed by e-mail hosts (AOL.com, Gmail.com, Yahoo.com, etc.) decide which mail is to be delivered and which is flagged as spam. Unless a prospect is expecting your e-mail, your message may never be opened.

Still, e-mail has its good points. A person may request to see printed materials as a follow-up to electronic communication. Chapter 6 explains electronic newsletters and the role they play in aiding your sales effort. The same is true for offering direct mail information and catalogs to readers of your online newsletter. Anyone who requests a mailed offer trades his or her e-mail address and other valuable details in exchange for receiving printed material. This is a smart prospecting tool for any marketer looking to capture as much information about their newsletter readers as possible.

Wikipedia: http://en.wikipedia.org/wiki/Spammer. ClickZ.com: www.clickz.com/stats/sectors/email/article.php/3580291.

cost. You can work with a graphic designer who will ensure that your brochures include pictures as well as text, or you can select an online printer that will let you create your own products and ship them to your doorstep just in time to begin your marketing campaign.

Words That Make Direct Mail Memorable

Emotion sells. It's that simple. Put yourself in the clients' shoes. Understand how they feel about a situation they're facing. What will you say to bring a sense of calm or satisfaction? What will relieve their fear or anxiety? These are the words that convince the prospect to buy.

You may be a pro at saying the right words but weak at putting those words on paper. If that's true, there are several places to find the words and phrases you need to craft your letters and other direct mail pieces:

Infomercials. There's no reason to reinvent the wheel when infomercials are filled with ideas and phrases to bring customers to your door. Videotape the commercials that, in your opinion, do the best job at raising product awareness and closing the sale. Write down key sentences and add them to your brainstorming list.

Junk mail. Why wrack your brain to put words together when professional copy editors send you materials daily through regular mail? Most direct mail letters are two pages in length, and the envelope often includes a promotional message that you can rewrite for your own use. Review each piece of mail you receive. Extract and edit the sentences that get your attention and that you believe will keep prospects reading your materials.

Advertorials in magazines and on the Internet. Sales copy is everywhere, including in print at these two locations. Magazine ads state the word "advertorial" at the top of each ad page, and it's easy to find this type of sales material on the Internet. Just look for single page sites that seem to scroll down for miles. These pages are created to sell books, manuals, reports, training CDs, or audiotapes on a specific subject. Anything that mirrors the message you wish to convey can be considered grist for rewrites for your own sales copy.

The real work starts once you've collected sentences and other ideas. You must change phrases so you don't plagiarize other people's work. Don't worry—there are enough words in the English language to shape your sales copy. Changing verbs and sentences to conform to what you sell will become second nature over time. This rewriting is not difficult. Write your text using comfortable language, words that string together easily when talking face-to-face with a potential customer. Unless your prospect is in your business, try not to use jargon or industry words, or you may lose the chance to convert the person from prospect to client in the first paragraph.

Look at this example of how to change a sentence to suit your sales needs.

Sentences from mailed sales copy:

"You know opportunity when you see it. That's why you started doing business online."

Sentences after changes:

"You don't need another opportunity to do business online. You need a better one that gets you up and running in less time."

Your direct mail copy must reveal your product's benefits and strengths and, in some cases, a guarantee or money-back offer to seal the deal. Free offers and other incentives help change a "maybe" into "yes." Such offers include:

- Thirty-minute trial consultation
- Free evaluation
- Credits in points or money upon order or subscription
- Free shipping in one or both directions
- Complimentary account analysis
- Free report by mail or e-mail
- Free CD or DVD
- Free checkup of old or current system

Any of these items sweeten your offer. Only you know what converts a person sitting on the fence into a buyer. Note, however, that such incentives cannot be offered on a regular basis or they will lose their effectiveness. Many solo business owners introduce their firm by offering something new and different in addition to the main product. Perhaps a certain month is slow for business, and a free offer acts to generate interest. Some industries, due to customization or product limitations, cannot offer add-ons. Instead they opt to maintain a level of exceptional service. You will learn about options by reviewing industry magazines, Web sites maintained by leaders and competitors, and direct mail literature and by networking with other industry participants.

Let's review the types of direct mail pieces that complement your Web site and review the reasons why you should consider each form of contact.

Letters

A letter is an assembly of words arranged in paragraphs that introduces your business to prospects in hopes of making a sale. Letters may not rate high on your list of direct mail tools. Perhaps that's because you've yet to receive a letter that made you take immediate action.

Letters produce sales. That's why millions of companies use this basic sales tool to connect with prospects worldwide. Letters are still considered one of the most inexpensive ways to sell. The part that takes the most time is crafting the content. Once the letter is written, you create a mailing list, run labels, insert the letter into the envelope, and mail. Creating the letter can be outsourced to a copywriter, but that's a pricey alternative. That's why using the language from other sales letters and recasting it into your own words is a smart strategy for the small-business owner.

You can print, stuff, and mail the letters yourself, or these tasks can be outsourced to a virtual assistant or other trusted source. Some home-based business owners ask friends to help when mailings add up to a thousand pieces or more. When the work is done, the owner hosts a small party in appreciation, which can also turn into a network gathering or a brainstorming session focused around the completed work.

Determining which type of letter to send a customer is just as important as its content. Some letters are straightforward, providing information and benefits on one or several pages. Some add humor to make a point. Other letters work in conjunction with postcards, reply cards, and other devices to encourage the prospect to take the requested action. Yet other letters act as a test for similar types of correspondence to be used in the future. If letters you receive by mail don't convince you to buy, that's no reason why you should neglect letters as a tool to connect with customers. Simply gather the best ideas from those same letters and then rewrite them into ones that will ultimately bring you sales.

Different Letters for Different Clients

Not all customers should receive the same letter. This is an important point. Tailor the introductions and endings to your prospects' characteristics. Large corporations segment their letters according to gender, geographic location, preferences, and other reasons. You may not be able to make hundreds of changes to one letter, but it is wise to make small changes, mailing two or three different formats according to the goals you hope to achieve. (As you will see in chapter 4, this same segmenting is applied to news releases, which are customized according to the media that receive them.)

Start by differentiating a letter's content and structure. In each case the first paragraph must instantly connect with a need or problem the reader is experiencing. That will keep him intrigued and wanting to learn more about solutions you offer.

On the next page is a sample letter that Janet Ross, the CPA featured in chapter 1, uses to introduce her business to prospects. This letter was created using ideas and information found in several direct mail pieces, mostly service businesses selling insurance, software, and infomercial products. Accounting is serious business, so Janet must use a straightforward approach to get attention.

The term "direct mail" implies how the correspondence is expected to arrive: by traditional means that includes an envelope (unless the correspondence is a postcard) and stamp to ensure delivery. But the word "direct" also focuses on getting the person's attention with words that uncover what she may be experiencing at the present time. Here's how Ross's letter gets its point across.

1. *Familiarity.* The first paragraph quotes a conversation that parallels a problem the reader understands. You hope to make a connection by having the reader say to herself, "Yes, I have that problem, too," and keep reading to learn how to solve it.
2. *Who you are.* Introduce your company as the firm willing and able to solve the

Dear   :

   "It's hard to find an accountant who watches my finances and helps me keep as much money as possible," a woman told me today by phone, "especially since I can't keep up with all the financial options."

   Do you have the same problem? AccountAble solves this and much more. We are dedicated to keeping your business in the black while you concentrate on the work you do best.

   As an experienced CPA who specializes in small and one-person businesses, I make my company's services available on a monthly or hourly basis. You may only need to contact us two times a year to review your books and make recommendations. This is what many of our clients prefer and why I encourage you to consider this very flexible option.

   My information kit will give you the full story. The kit can be accessed on the Internet at www.webpageurl.com. Or return the enclosed reply card, and I'll send you a free kit describing how we can work to keep more money in your pocket for reinvesting, retirement, and other needs.

   Whether you're satisfied with your current accountant or are thinking of making a change, I urge you to visit www.webpageurl.com or respond with the enclosed reply card. There's no obligation, and your satisfaction is always guaranteed.

   From experience, I've learned that the best time to evaluate an accountant is before you need one, not when tax time is just around the corner. Let us show you how AccountAble makes keeping your profits simple and easy.

Sincerely,
Janet Ross
CPA and Profitability Counselor

PS: Trying to decide which accounting software is best for you? Call me at (303) 555-2345 for a 15-minute, no-obligation discussion to learn your options.

problem. If you are in the same locale as the prospect, that can also be mentioned early in the correspondence, or you can add that fact in another part of the letter. A local solution, in some industries, is viewed by many as an asset.

3. *Experience.* Everyone wants a problem solver with a track record. Customize your letter with satisfaction gained from people in the same business structure (sole proprietorship, partnership, etc.) or industry.

4. *Flexibility.* Some prospects will have deep pockets and be able to pay any amount of money for what you offer. Others need sporadic help or a plan that fits their budget. Be sure to mention this in your pitch.

5. *Action.* Tell the reader what to do to initiate contact. Action ranges from making a phone call, sending an e-mail, visiting your Web site, coming into the office for a complimentary product or service, or mailing a postage-paid card. Direct mail readers need guidance; without it your mailing will be deposited directly into the trash.

6. *Finale.* A postscript, or PS, beneath your signature is said to be an effective reminder tool of an important point mentioned within the letter. That's why it's found in most, if not all, direct mail correspondence. A postscript can also be used to add a secondary offer.

All direct mail letters are created using one or more of these points, arranged in a manner that connects with readers. Janet's letter is one page in length. She knows that her prospects are time-stressed business owners, people who shy away from reading long-winded dissertations. A one-page letter identifies the problem and solution.

Other products or services may require up to four pages of explanation. For example, a newsletter publisher must document the reasons why an industry-specific newsletter costs $495 a year. The publication's features are identified using bulleted points, case studies, and endorsements from industry leaders. The hefty price tag calls for a healthy explanation of benefits.

Roger Green, chapter 1's golf equipment owner, could have taken the serious approach to reach potential customers. But because of the characteristics of his industry, he chooses to go the light-hearted route. The letter on the next page shows what he plans to mail as an introduction.

Green's letter effectively grabs the reader's attention. However, there are marked differences from Janet Ross's letter due to the casual approach and competitive tone. The letter on the next page shows how it connects with the prospect.

1. *Focus.* Feet, one body part that gets a work-out on the golf course, is the addressee. Beauty salons may address a person's hair. A caterer's or tea shop's target is taste buds. Whatever body part is the main focus, within reason, is prime target for addressing within your letter.

Dear Mr. Hanson's Feet,

We don't often take the time to address other feet. But our concern is for your comfort, and that's what prompted us to contact you.

It seems that other golf retailers aren't giving you what you need: one place to find supplies, equipment, and individual training to keep your game at its best during match play and casual outings. But there's one retailer that is. Teed Up is the company to call rather than spend your time driving from retail shop to retail shop and speaking with salespeople who know little about you or golf.

At your convenience and at no obligation, we'll bring the golf course to you. You'll see a selection of golf products that fits your size and experience, all in the comfort of your home or office, and hear about our specialized instruction that keeps your game on par and on the green.

Other retailers seem to have cold feet about making your life easier by bringing golf product choices directly to you. Or maybe they're just dragging their feet. Who knows?

The next time you're ready to aim for a score of 60, remember that Teed Up is the **only** golf product and training facility that provides in-office service. We'll even bring you a pair of socks and foot powder so you'll be ready for long hours on the golf course.

Call us at (704) 555-6568 for a closer look at the products and services that will make you stretch, shake, and stay on par. Again, the appointment is complimentary—there is absolutely no obligation.

Also be sure to check out the enclosed "foot note" that explains our Tutorial of the Month program and business buyers' incentives.

Sincerely,
Roger Green
Teed Up's Head Golfologist

2. *Strengths.* Others selling the same products and their weaknesses are mentioned and compared to your strengths. This is handled effectively without divulging competitive names. A laundry list of limitations is unnecessary; just one or two examples make the point.

3. *Convenience.* Bringing your wares to the reader, rather than having him come to you, is a premium in today's society. Any time-saving strategies and one-stop shopping advantages should always be mentioned.

4. *Incentive.* Make sure that perks complement the package. In this example, socks and foot powder are gifts presented during the initial meeting because the reader's feet are the addressee. If using a straightforward letter, a package of tees or golf balls is just as valuable.

5. *Closing.* "Call us" is the preferred action. This lets the reader and you connect so that the best choice of products accompanies you to the home or office. Other options may not uncover as many facts as provided during a phone call.

6. *Enclosures.* A brochure is added in an attempt to gain the reader's confidence and trust. This reference tool serves to confirm details mentioned in the letter and leads him to a Web site for more information. The letter's last paragraph is appropriate, but it could have been used as a footnote or postscript.

An offbeat letter can win results, but stay within smart boundaries when ending the correspondence. Roger Green will sign his name in pen rather than add a footprint above his name. So should you.

Here are more ideas to begin and end your letters, taken from random direct mail correspondence.

Beginnings

"You don't need another _____, you need a better one."

"As soon as you say so, I'll send you ____."

"Now you can get _____ for pennies a day."

Closings

"Your satisfaction is our top priority."

"If you're not pleased, we will refund your money and cancel all fees."

"This offer is available for a limited time, so act now."

Postcards

It is said that prospects take time to digest both sides of a postcard. That's because there's nothing to open, and its size accommodates a limited number of words, making it a means of disseminating information quickly and easily. Most business owners who mail postcards add a photograph or graphic image on one side, which grabs the attention of anyone who handles the item, including postal service employees. These are just a few reasons why postcards are adored by home-based and solo business owners. Here are three more reasons.

1. Cost factors make postcards affordable in any budget.
2. Creation takes less time than other types of correspondence.
3. Small amounts can be generated with your computer and printer, while larger quantities are outsourced to commercial printers or the many online postcard specialists worldwide.

There was no way I could work with a commercial printer in the early 1990s to create the type of postcards I wanted to distribute. Printers in my area didn't have the ability to produce a slick, glossy card. Everything was finished with a matte surface, which meant my message would arrive with an uninviting appearance. I would have wasted my time and money. My only outlet was to create postcards using my own computer and printer. Can you imagine using a Kaypro computer, dot matrix printer, and scored four-by-six-inch cards fed through the printer with a pin connection on either side? That's what I did. Whatever method that was available to make contact with the people most interested in what I sold was fair game.

Postcards either work in conjunction with other direct mail tools or they work alone to remind prospects and clients of your existence. For example, a marketer sends a letter of introduction along with an offer or incentive. Two weeks later a postcard is mailed to those same targets as a reminder of the letter. A second postcard, mailed two weeks after the first, ends this particular campaign by recommending a product or service and steering the reader to a Web site for more information. Aside from the cost for stationery products, 93 cents ($.41 + $.26 + $.26 = $.93) was used for postage instead of the $1.23 it would have cost to mail three letters. That may not seem like a huge sum of money, but multiply the 30-cent savings by the number of postcards you currently send or will mail in the future. The reduced expense keeps money available for more products and campaigns.

Postcard suppliers on the Web have gained popularity with home-based business owners and large corporations who need a simple product that draws lots of attention and ultimately many sales. Online suppliers have drawn criticism when the product isn't made to the buyers' specifications, but that's true of other postcard makers. Office supply retailers and local printers don't always get the order right, but their mishaps aren't as publicized on Internet message boards and blogs as those businesses with Web prominence.

If postcards are an option that fits into your marketing strategy, here are your design choices as well as their pros and cons.

Make Them Yourself

Designing your own postcards is relatively simple. It's more expensive than ordering preprinted

FREE SHIPPING IN AUGUST

Save this month at
GiftBasketBusiness.com when you
order any of our sales-building products.

During August, shipping is free*!

Order through the secure site, or
call us today at (800) 555-0000 and a
representative will assist you.

**www.sweetsurvival.com/gbstore/
nfoscomm/catalog/**

*Shipping is free throughout the U.S.

Choose From:

- Books, Product Guides
- VHS, DVDs, Audiotapes
- Single State Directories
- Starter Kits
- Marketing Tools
- Booklets
- Bow-making Help
- Letter Writing Support
- Find more on our site

postcards from an outside source, but if you have a mailing of a hundred prospects to receive a unique message and the minimum card order from a supplier is 250, the self-produced card option is ideal. What's needed to create your postcards are a computer, a laser or an ink-jet printer, postcard template software, and a hundred unprinted postcards.

Avery: www.avery.com. Microsoft: www .microsoft.com

Templates can be found on the Web through companies such as Avery, the well-known label manufacturer that also sells its unprinted postcards in office supply stores. The template area on Microsoft's Web site features dozens of postcard templates. Postcard-making software is found in retail stores bundled with a host of other options, but, there's no reason to spend money on a product that can be downloaded by computer.

Self-published postcards are a great tool for alerting customers about a special offer, announcing your appearance at a forthcoming local function, or giving notice about an upcoming event.

Pros. Great for printing small quantities. Easy to change the appearance or message.

Cons. Appearance may look cheap to some recipients. Drains printer ink if full-size color photos are added. Cost per postcard can be twice as much as ordering from a supplier.

Internet Suppliers

Web-based business card suppliers usually make postcards, too. Template choices are extensive, allowing you to select color or black-and-white images that draw attention when the card is retrieved from mailboxes. That's the one part of the postcard that cannot be accomplished expertly through your own printer. These postcard prices are affordable, and the price per postcard decreases as the order quantity increases.

While some Internet suppliers make every imaginable image available for one side of your postcard, others have the ability to capture your Web site's home page or blog, making it the postcard image. Such a postcard can be used to introduce or reintroduce your site, promote a new section, or tell clients about new products. Best of all, an image of your Web site or blog will be unique when it arrives by mail.

There are dozens of postcard suppliers on the Web. Review as many suppliers' sites as possible before committing the time to creating your perfect postcard. Read the FAQ sections to learn about the postcard quality (thickness, coatings, etc.) and types of available finishes (matte, glossy, etc.). From there, you'll be able to compare postcards on an apple-to-apple basis rather than just by price.

Pros. Abundant suppliers on the Web. Quick turnaround from creation to delivery. Other marketing products available from the same source. Large selection of stock images. Easy-to-use templates on most sites. Some provide extra services, such as mailing your postcards when they're ready.

Cons. Templates difficult to customize on some sites. No-refund policies make rechecking work imperative. Postcheckout options increase the total cost if you're not careful. Some sites share your information with third parties (check each Web site's FAQ and terms of service).

Commercial Printers

Gone are the days of massive two-color machines tended by printers who lacked flair and creativity. They've been replaced by graphic artists with Macintosh computers and the ability to take your artwork from conception to completion. These individuals, who are part artist, part printer, make themselves visible at local networking groups and business gatherings, often sponsoring an event in exchange for time to showcase what they do best.

Commercial printers are found in all regions, and it seems best to use one that's in your local area unless one outside of your region is highly recommended. Ask professionals within your circle for leads. When a person presents you with a remarkable promotional product, remember to ask who created it. You may discover a commercial source in your area that you did not know existed. Another option is to use your local Yellow Pages or to type the words "commercial printer" along with your state or city name in an Internet search engine.

Pros. In-house graphic artists create visually appealing, one-of-a-kind postcards that can't be matched elsewhere. Local source builds another great relationship and your at-large network.

Cons. It may take lots of time to create and print your postcards. Start the creation process early. Price may be more than online sources.

Retail Office Suppliers

The same place that sells paper and pencils also supplies postcards ready to send by mail. This is the retail outlet that sells the unprinted postcards that you design on your own mentioned earlier under "Make Them Yourself." Go to the store's copy center. You'll find a thick, spiral-bound book filled with pages of logos and colors that can be printed on business cards, postcards, and other quick-to-make promotional pieces. Your order is outsourced to another firm that subcontracts to the office supply store. You won't find any dazzling products here, but what the store offers may be suitable for you.

➤ Staples: www.staples.com. OfficeMax: www.officemax.com. Office Depot: www.officedepot.com.

As with every other type of postcard supplier, you must make sure that your preferred image and all of the information to be contained on the postcard is added to the order form. The store representative is assisting you, but don't place your faith in that person. These are *your* postcards, so review the order carefully before applying your signature and making payment.

Pros. Regional location makes access easy and convenient. Books readily available at the copy or printing area to find what you want. Products are good for tradespeople, especially plumbers and electricians.

Cons. Very limited postcard choices. Vanilla appearance; nothing custom or outstanding.

United States Postal Service (USPS)

U.S.-based post offices handle mail that travels worldwide, with the exception of packages mailed to certain countries and hazardous materials traveling anywhere. But they do handle one

Shirley Says

Quick Postcards to the Rescue

I use the services of online postcard suppliers, but I also continue to create my own. Sometimes I need to print a quantity of twenty-four or forty-eight with a message that's limited to one mailing. When that's the focus, I turn to unprinted postcards sold in packs by office suppliers. They're available in small (four four-by-six-inch postcards per sheet) or large (two five-by-eight-inch postcards per sheet) formats, both in eight-and-one-half-by-eleven-inch sizes, the same as a regular sheet of paper so it feeds through your laser or inkjet printer. I use the smaller postcards. For me they're efficient, and the postage stays low while delivering my custom message. The larger postcards make a big impact as they travel from point A to point B, but the cost is the same as a business-size letter. Because of that, I'd rather use the small ones, but don't let me influence which postcard to select. Choose the product that's best for your marketing campaign. The larger postcards seem to be popular because they sell briskly at stores. Perhaps they'll also work to enhance your promotions.

item that your competitors consider "hazardous," and that's your direct mail. The USPS not only distributes premade, stamped postcards, they also create and mail them.

One of my California-based friends mailed me a postcard that was created, stamped, and shipped by the USPS. The postcard acted as a promotion, with my friend explaining, on the card, how the USPS can provide the same service for me. It opened my eyes to an alternative to other postcard vendors. It also unleashed a barrage of questions:

- How easy is it?
- Can it all be done online?
- Are there templates from which to choose designs?
- Is there a quantity limit?
- What's the cost?

➤ United States Postal Service: www.usps .com/netpost/.

I went to the USPS site to find out more. It couldn't hurt to learn about another option that takes the work out of my hands. USPS offers postcards, through a third party, in color or black-and-white formats. Regular (one-sided black-and-white image, matte finish) and premium (one- or two-sided color image, glossy finish) formats are offered. Two postcard sizes are available, and you can track your order at any time. There is a production charge for each order, starting at $2, and the cost for each postcard is said to be as low as the price for a first-class stamp. USPS provides an online calculator to learn how much your mailing will cost.

As an example, a small postcard (four-by six-inches) printed on one side in black and white is $.302 each. The same postcard size printed in color on two sides is $.437 each. The mailing service expands to include letters, brochures, flyers, greeting and gift cards, and newsletters, making direct mail available in every format.

Postcards through USPS are customizable. For other products you must send a file with specifications to ensure that your correspondence is set up correctly. Your internal mailing list is another file that's required to put your message into customers' mailboxes. The USPS Web site will inform you of the best way to send this documentation.

This service is beneficial for many home-based and solo business owners with mailing lists that are so large that it takes days to complete a mailing.

Having a service such as the USPS take care of all the work is more than a question of money. You must also consider how much time it takes to design, place the order, add address labels, stamp postcards, and drive them to the post office for mailing. Those hours can be an enormous drain on time and resources; when someone else can do this work, you can concentrate on other aspects of your marketing plan. Think about that before disregarding the USPS option or other alternatives offered by postcard suppliers.

Newspaper Subscription Flyers

Did you know that local publishers will create a flyer, reproduce it, insert it into newspapers set for home delivery, and deliver it for you on a specified day, all for a nominal fee? If homeowners who subscribe to newspaper delivery are part of your target market, this is a great opportunity to make a connection with them. Think about it: You're a landscaper, plumber, or home cleaning specialist with plans to grow your customer base. You need a method to reach customers. Flyers placed within home-delivered newspapers may be your best route.

I learned about this process through a newspaper flyer added to my own home-delivered paper. It advertised the creation and distribution of 1,000 flyers for $700. Reaching 1,000 or more households at a rate of seventy cents per home is a bargain for some, especially those who offer a product or service for homeowners. One lead may net you ten times more than the promotion's cost.

This direct mail service is valuable because of other factors:

1. Flyers are sent only to subscribers and are not inserted in papers sold at newsstands. Sporadic newsstand buying would make your marketing campaign hit and miss, depending on who bought the paper on that day.
2. Promotions added to weekend editions, including your flyer, are more likely to be reviewed by subscribers in a leisurely manner. The newspaper's contents are scanned thoroughly on the weekend; during the week readers are more preoccupied and don't have time to consider your offer.
3. Publishers provide you with many distribution options, such as delivery to specific zip codes or homes rather than apartments. This type of segmenting is similar to what Yellow Page representatives offer when selling ads in certain telephone books.

A newspaper flyer is as basic as it sounds. It's one sheet of letter-size paper, printed on one side with details about your product, service, or promotion. It may include a photographic image that tells readers, in an instant, the type of product you are promoting. A border may appear about one inch from all sides. The flyer will not be a full-color product, especially for the price, but it may be printed on color paper. A newspaper account executive will be able to send or show you samples of other flyers. Samples might also be available online.

Visit your local newspaper's Web site to find information about promotional flyers, or call the advertising department for details. Perhaps your local paper offers the service but only on a limited basis, or maybe it has never offered the service but will work with you to create a flyer that's inserted into home deliveries. Most large newspapers are owned by conglomerates that have a flyer distribution service. If you've never seen a flyer in your local paper, it means one of two things: 1) You don't receive the home delivery edition, or 2) no company in your area has taken advantage of this low-cost distribution service.

Clean Your Chimney Today!

Does your family breathe poisonous air all winter long because the chimney is clogged? What's up there that's harming your loved ones?

Clean Sweep Chimney Cleaners will remove debris, dead animals, and hazardous materials from your chimney. We'll install a new grate on top to keep cleanliness in and animals out. Don't wait any longer. Make an appointment today. Your family's good health depends on it.

CLEAN SWEEP CHIMNEY CLEANERS
Call (904) 555-CLOG

Winter Special!
Call by September 15 and pay just $99.95.
Free gift with every cleaning.

Although newspaper subscription flyers don't arrive in the prospect's mailbox, they are part of a direct delivery service that may stand out from letters. It's an alternative to consider if your service benefits the local community.

Surveys

Business is going well. Clients seem to respond positively to the range of products and services offered by your firm. But is something missing? Is there an ancillary service that will clinch their loyalty? Does another company make ordering easier? A survey reveals the answers, providing solutions that self-brainstorming cannot uncover.

Sending a survey by mail gives you another reason to connect with customers, but this time they have a chance to tell you what they think. Everyone wants a say. Clients will be happy to provide input as long as you follow rules that they've set for satisfaction.

1. Determine the survey's focus so you get the most from the interaction. It's permissible to ask questions on a variety of areas. Perhaps you're about to launch a new product, or you plan to follow up on a service plan, or you need to know if a competitor's product is of interest to customers. All of these points can be addressed in your survey, but try to stay within limits.

2. Ask no more than twelve questions. Like you, clients have little time to respond. Choose the twelve most influential queries.

If more than twelve are needed, stay within the limits of one sheet of paper.

3. Make the answer choices specific. "Yes" and "no" responses yield no ideas or solutions. Rather than ask, "Is the pie tart?" ask, "How would you describe the pie's flavor?" or "Describe the pie's flavor," followed by the answers: a) sweet, b) tart, c) bland, d) no flavor. This example has been simplified; answers in sentence structure are better for most surveys. In addition, include the word "other" and a blank line as an extra answer option for each question. This gives clients the opportunity to express themselves and to offer insights that you may not have anticipated.

4. Use the last questions to gather statistics about the respondents, such as gender, profession or industry affiliation, and geographic location. This will help you to find more clients with similar traits.

5. Give a deadline for submission. Most clients will submit surveys on time. A deadline will ensure that the largest quantity of submissions arrives by a specific date.

6. Offer an incentive, something that shows your gratitude for completing the survey on time. Incentives are anything from a discounted service to a gift card or other products. Most of all, the offer must be valuable to clients but affordable for you. Ask colleagues for incentive advice, and consult magazines that focus on the incentive

industry to find a suitable trade-off that benefits both you and your client. (Turn to chapter 9 for an in-depth discussion about incentives.)

↖ *Incentive* magazine: www.incentivemag.com. *Potentials:* www.potentialsmag.com.

Before the advent of Web sites, surveys were strictly sent by direct mail. It's still advisable to send your questionnaire by traditional means. Mail your survey and include a postage-paid envelope. How often have you received a survey with no incentive notification or postage on the envelope? I can't tell you the number of times such mail has been sent to me, but I can confirm that none of them were completed. You need this information, so invest in round-trip delivery.

The survey's introduction is placed at the top of the page, before the survey questions begin. If you wish to notify clients that the survey is also available on your Web site, tell them in the introduction so they're aware of the delivery options. If clients are Web savvy, they'll appreciate taking the survey online. Sending a text incentive immediately after the survey is completed is also beneficial. I've dispensed online questionnaires using software that allowed me to send an e-mailed document in PDF format to clients as long as their e-mail address was entered properly in a specific box.

Surveys can be created as part of your Web site, or distribution is available through firms that let you create surveys online. Some online survey companies are free to use, but the free option comes with its own price: There are often limits on the number of questions as well as limits on responses. Other companies charge a fee for creation tools and enhanced services. These tools are viewed as gold by home-based business owners who need help with response numbers and other statistics available through paid sources.

How often should you employ surveys?

Query your clients in eighteen-month to two-year intervals. Surveys distributed more frequently may cause SFS (survey fatigue syndrome). SFS is punishable by clients who vow to never again complete your questionnaires, open your mail, or visit your Web site. Surveys allow customers to provide you with ideas and insights that keep your company on the cutting edge. Ask clients occasional questions, but do not treat them like full-time employees.

Newsletters

Postcards give clients quick updates and announcements. Newsletters are structured to give a more in-depth look into how a business connects products and services with customers. They feature multiple articles on product uses, customer profiles, problems and solutions, trends, and more. Online newsletters, discussed in chapter 6, are delivered on a weekly, bimonthly, or monthly basis. The direct mail counterpart arrives monthly or quarterly. Why should you consider publishing both a direct mail and an online newsletter?

Online version

1. Complements the Web site, leading readers to areas online related to articles or tips.
2. Helps to increase secure shopping cart revenue.
3. Encourages readers to subscribe to the print version.
4. Increases blog postings and readership.

Direct mail version

1. Print component is read by clients who prefer text by mail.
2. Created using online version's ideas.
3. Clients often keep printed version as reference material.
4. Acts as an income producer if subscription fee is required.

I still have copies of my first newsletter, which was published in the mid-1990s. The eight-page publication was created by computer using newsletter software. I printed the sixteen pages on my printer and laid out the format for duplication at an office supply retailer, where public copying machines were available. The newsletter was published on eleven-by-seventeen-inch lavender-colored paper folded in half and saddle stitched to make the publication look neat and professional. Subscribers paid $12 a year to receive my news.

This print newsletter continued for several years before I decided to add an online component. Then I stopped the text newsletter because of the time needed to complete the project compared to the revenue it generated. Some industries thrive with both print and online newsletters, while other industries survive on just one version. Unless your newsletter is sponsored by industry corporations, direct mail newsletters require subscription fees to cover creation costs. This is a blanket statement; however, I don't know of any solo business owners who make a print publication available at no charge. It seems that the more your products or services cost, the more coveted the newsletter—and therefore you can charge a bundle to create it. Lower-revenue industries cannot capture enough subscribers, so online versions are easier to create and stay in line with budgets.

If a printed newsletter holds the key to generating promotion and sales, there are ways to create that newsletter that keep you out of the office supply store waiting for your turn at the copier.

Industry Affiliations

In chapter 1, Janet Ross's marketing plan includes contacting two companies that create newsletters for accounting professionals. Such firms take care of the setup and distribution, placing Janet's name and her firm's information on the newsletter as if she were the person who created the publication. There may be a similar option for you. Industry publications, colleagues, and trade show exhibitors may be of service in locating an outsourcing service.

USPS

As mentioned in the earlier discussion of post-cards, the U.S. Postal Service creates newsletters. Visit its Web site for site area and other information with details on this service.

Online Sources

Type the words "newsletter creation" or "newsletter printing" in a search engine to find companies that provide this service. Companies still exist to create your customized newsletter because they recognize the need to reach customers who don't consider Internet-based products to be their sole or main news source.

Business owners in many industries successfully use printed newsletters as a direct mail tool. Hopefully you can do the same.

Note Cards

Note cards are a direct mail product that I highly recommend as part of your marketing arsenal. Sending cards to clients in appreciation of past business, for birthday or other greetings, or mailed in place of postcards and flyers will set you head and shoulders above competitors and others who sell just about anything. Note card greetings occur less frequently between client and service provider. It's becoming a lost art, but you can breathe new life into this simple technique that spreads positive word about your business around town and throughout the world.

My first note cards were made by the printer that created my stationery. I ordered a large quantity and am still using the same batch. A note card is included with every order mailed to clients. It expresses appreciation and good wishes for a successful business. If a client orders a second or third time, I search my customer database to make sure the message in the new card states something different from the first. It takes less than two minutes to write the note card, but I measure the connection in goodwill fostered rather than in time spent.

When I travel to speak at trade shows, many clients who have received my note cards thank me in person. Others say that the cards are posted in their offices as good luck symbols. I am honored and pleased to send this small token of appreciation. After all, the people who buy from me can always decide to work with someone else. Sending a note card with each order is the least I can do for clients ordering an average of $80 per sale.

Note cards are available through many sources. They can be made by the same printer that created your stationery, ensuring that you have matching products to create a brand statement when contacting customers. Cards are available as a custom order through retail stationery firms. You can also buy different packs of note cards from retailers located worldwide.

Note cards need not be filled with world-renowned prose. Simply use words that remind, connect, inspire, or comfort. Two lines of text are appropriate, but sometimes you'll find yourself turning the note card to the back side to finish your thoughts.

TOP INSIDE OF NOTE CARD

June 28, 2007

Dear Sarah,

Just a quick note to thank you for considering our services. Busy professionals such as you need to stay focused on projects that increase revenue. I hope you'll consider us to concentrate on your profitability.

Wishing you success in business,

Janet Ross
AccountAble

How many note cards do you receive in a month? You can probably count the number on one hand and have five fingers left. Taking the time to write a note tells the receiver that you're the type of person who deserves to stay within reach. Aside from sending note cards to clients, I often use cards to connect with good friends, industry professionals, and other people I meet in my travels. I sent note cards to people I take to lunch, treat me to lunch, talk with me while flying, speak with me by phone, share a story after my speaking engagement, or act as my therapist when I complain about a business or personal problem.

There are people in your circle of friends, family members, and colleagues who do nice things for you as well as clients who deserve attention with a handwritten note. If you have no cards or cannot find a retailer with something special, look for a package at a supermarket or discount store. It doesn't matter where the cards are purchased. What matters is that the note card is prepared, signed, and mailed. That's the type of direct mail that separates you from all others.

Direct mail is a simple process that uses many forms of printed materials to introduce your business and stay connected with clients. Select the formats that realistically fit within your marketing strategy. Then use these tactics to dazzle everyone who connects with you, turning them into loyal and satisfied colleagues and clients.

04

Maximum Attention through Print Media Coverage

Getting press coverage in the local newspaper must be easy. After all, Hal's Hardware and Scrapbook City always get featured, so how hard can it be? Your business is much better than theirs. The local editor will spring into action after she receives a call and hears why your product is the best invention since sliced bread. She'll reserve tomorrow's front page to tell everyone what you sell, where you're located, and why your business is great. The phone will start ringing, and Internet sales will pour in. You'll become a millionaire all because of that one phone call. It doesn't get any better than that.

Such dreams do come true, but not instantaneously. You're about to embark on a journey into media relations, the all-important world that connects your business with individuals and corporations that will soon become customers, hopefully on a long-term basis. The media work as a close ally, broadcasting your message in print, e-mail, audio, video, and electronic formats—as long as you follow certain rules. Finding the right media sources takes time and patience. This chapter shows you how to uncover news outlets and how to make the right impression with reporters and editors who will broadcast your news across town and around the world. Then chapter 5 will take your media relations one step further—onto radio, TV, and cable.

You won't make a call one day and be in print the next, but you will make inroads slowly and surely until newspapers and on-air reports seem incomplete without your name, at least on a local level.

These are the main steps that produce media coverage.

- Create a list of ideas to send to news sources.
- Write a news release tailored to the intended audience.
- Decide who receives your releases and how to contact them.
- Choose several news distribution options.
- Use a checklist to document distribution formats and results.

Now you're ready to learn about media coverage, where making news and securing relationships has the potential to bring you so much promotion that your dreams just might come true.

An Introduction to News Releases

Rumors tend to be accurate, but the following one is off base, according to the editors who speak at media events. It says that the traditional news release is dead, that the media are no longer interested in this decades-old distribution format for educating, informing, and notifying readers about businesses locally and worldwide. There's no word on what is supposedly taking the news release's place, and that fact proves that the news release still reigns as the instrument to distribute business information in print, on television, and through Web circulation.

FYI: News release definitions. Wikipedia: http://en.wikipedia.org/wiki/News_release. PRNewswire: http://prntoolkit.prnewswire.com/ PRNewswire/faqs/what1.shtml.

A news release, also known as a press release, informs the media about a newsworthy event that promotes your business. A release is created for any number of reasons, from securing a new client to donating products to sponsoring an event. It can provide tips to educate potential buyers or shatter myths associated with your industry.

A basic news release may be structured in the following format. The first paragraph explains the main reason for the news. The second paragraph includes a quote from you or another credible source. The third paragraph provides statistics or expands on details mentioned in the first paragraph. The last paragraph states your company's credentials and contact information.

Not all news releases follow this pattern, but the outline gives you a good plan to follow as you begin creating your news. On the next page is a press release submitted to the media during a crisis in the southwestern portion of the United States. It was published in local newspapers where the fires occurred.

Your news must contain details that inform an editor why it is relevant to the reader. The release's main focus is known as an "angle" or a "hook." It pinpoints why newspapers, magazines, and other media outlets should share your news with the world. The angle in the above release piggybacked off a current news topic, which is why the media viewed the content as timely.

Each release should contain only one angle,

FOR IMMEDIATE RELEASE

Contact: Shirley Frazier, Day/Evening (973) 279-2799

NEW REASON TO DOCUMENT VALUABLES BEFORE TRAGEDY STRIKES

Paterson, New Jersey (July 3, 2002)—What happens if your home or apartment is lost to a fire or flood, and there is no record of your valuables? That's the question homeowners and renters who are victims of the fires raging in Arizona and Colorado face today.

"Homeowners' journals are selling fast," says Shirley Frazier, president of Sweet Survival, a gift and gourmet consulting firm. "Property owners across the country are realizing the importance of listing their valuables, documenting serial numbers, and photographing their possessions, and then placing all of the information in one concise book," explains Frazier. "The journal should be updated each year and placed in a fireproof box at a secure facility outside of the home. That ensures that the journal's contents are preserved if tragedy strikes."

According to the National Fire Safety Board, more than 580,000 homes were destroyed in 2001, with insurance claims totaling $8.4 million. More than 10 percent of homeowners' claims are denied because there is no proof of ownership included with filings. Creating and storing a journal listing valuables and home improvements can increase claim approvals.

In business since 1990, Sweet Survival provides start-up and marketing assistance to entrepreneurs, retail store owners, and gift industry wholesalers. Shirley Frazier is an author and professional speaker who has won numerous business awards, appeared on CNBC, and is frequently quoted in trade and consumer magazines. For more information, contact Shirley Frazier at (973) 279-2799.

###

and a news release on a specific topic can be restructured for numerous media sources that print news from different angles. That's how successful promoters get their releases mentioned in more than one newspaper or magazine. It may seem like a lot of work. But if that's the way to get monthly exposure that attracts prospects and increases orders—all for the price of stamps and the time it takes to create and send your news—it's worth it.

If your business sells to retailers, wholesalers, and consumers, those three angles are your focus in three separate news releases. The first paragraph is revised to make each group the focal point. An example of how to change a release to create a new angle is shown later in the chapter.

I learned to create a news release through books in local libraries. My library is still a favorite hangout. Although the Internet is widely used as a research tool, books are considered to be a more credible source for information. The books I consulted provided in-depth tutorials on what to do and not do when creating a news release. I started submitting my news to my local newspaper, and I wrote several releases that weren't published. Library books warned me to expect very little or no press coverage at the beginning. It's a rite of passage you should expect, but don't let that deter you. An editor may file the news without your knowledge. Then one day a story develops that invites your participation.

The moment my news was featured in a newspaper column, I felt as if I had cleared a hurdle. My news release writing style became better, and the media rewarded me with many quotes and feature stories. Once you learn how to match your news with a current event or industry trend, the same will happen to you.

Why News Releases Are Vital to Business

Few activities provide as much media buzz as a news release, especially when it's tailored to match the media's specifications. It rates as high as networking or as creating a dynamic Web site that captures corporate or consumer interest.

Developing and submitting one news release every month has the potential to bring business to you in ways never imagined. Once you start to see the possibilities, submitting news stories will become as habit forming as the work you jump out of bed to do each day.

That said, it's easy to sink into a rut or become disinterested in creating your monthly press release. Everyone in business on their own experiences this type of temporary drought. However, when you win new accounts, sponsor a Little League team, or receive an award for businessperson of the year, that's the type of news that gets media attention. When you fail to write a release, you decrease the potential to attract new clients each month. You may not see it right away, but your profit-and-loss statement tells the story.

When I started my business, I was determined to get press coverage. One release, written about flavor trends in the gourmet industry, finally brought me the attention I craved—a front-page story with a large, color photo under the headline. Orders and additional publicity poured in. That's what can happen when you're patient. Here's a short list of what occurred as a result.

- A newspaper publisher ordered twelve Christmas gifts from me for staff members.
- An insurance agent requested 150 gifts for her clients.
- A Food Network producer called to book me as a guest.
- Several trade publications requested expert quotes for upcoming articles.

Subsequent articles were featured in trade publications and in a different section of the local newspaper that featured Mother's Day gift trends.

Once a newspaper prints a feature story or anything that includes you as a source, it's time to make the most of your temporary limelight. First, check the publication's Web site to see if the story is available online. If so, place a link to the story in your Web site. Simply copy and paste the article's online address and add a caption that highlights the link to your Web site's home page or another notable page, such as in your online media room. (We'll talk about creating a media room in chapter 5.)

Many newspapers keep articles available online only for a short period of time, so check the link once a month to make sure it's still accessible. It's okay to quote your part of the article in print or on your Web site as long as you attribute the quote to its original publication.

Making duplicate copies of news stories that feature your business is another smart idea. Include these copies with print materials you send to customers and media sources that request information by mail. That's one technique I used to convince the Food Network to schedule me as a guest.

Other ways to exploit your fifteen minutes of fame include:

- Using the transcript to elevate you as an industry expert (see chapter 5).

- Offering to speak to groups for fifteen to twenty minutes on your expertise, exposing you to a wider audience of interested buyers (chapter 5).

How to Determine What's Newsworthy

The information printed in daily newspapers reveals what the media consider important to readers. Very few papers will mention a grand opening unless it's part of a column where such announcements are welcome. When sending information to the media, your mission is to educate, inform, and explain to readers why what you sell is beneficial to them, their home, business, family members, or whatever the end users seek to make their personal or professional lives easier or better.

The products and services we sell take on a human quality when we talk about them. That's because to us they are living, breathing extensions of ourselves. But the language we use to describe our wares and the information sent to the media must tell a different story. For example, you may believe that your service is the "greatest" or "easiest" on the market, but such words will never be used in print by a credible journalist. I can guarantee that no one who interviews you in general media circles will add those flowery adjectives to a description. Remember that "newsworthiness" stresses timeliness and how your product or information benefits the public.

Here are ideas to create news that reporters prefer to print.

- How a product for newborns provides a restful sleep or teething relief.
- A sponsorship or donation to a local charity and why that group was chosen.
- A free in-store, office, or online contest, along with prize information and entrance details.
- An innovative way you're outsourcing business or hiring employees, and how it supports the community.
- A marketing option that's different from anything else being done in the area and the benefits that make it worthwhile.

My first news release, written in 1990, was poorly crafted even though I spent lots of time in the library researching how to create an exciting story. I wrote and submitted news every month and sent it to local editors covering business, lifestyle, home, and health sections. Most business owners understand that change comes gradually, and when attempting to attract the media, patience tends to wear thin over time. I knew the tide would turn and that an editor would call me, so I continued to submit what I hoped were better-written news releases.

Here's what the library books taught me.

1. Use plain, white paper rather than stationery when mailing your release. Editors receive lots of releases on colored paper, but plain paper stands out.
2. The body of the release must be in either one-and-a-half- or double-spaced format, and each paragraph should be indented.
3. Address your envelope to a specific editor. A generic title such as "The Editor" brands you as a person who is unwilling to research the correct person's name and therefore is not a candidate for news coverage.
4. Put the "who, what, why, where, when, and how" in the first paragraph, if possible. Editors scan mail quickly because they receive hundreds of releases each day. The important points should appear at the beginning to keep their interest. One exception to this rule is shown in the sample release on page 60, where the story starts with a human-interest focus. Nonetheless, the release still includes information about who, what, and where at the start.
5. Add the angle. Write the release in an informative style, not in an advertising format. If your news is about opening a store or having a sale, it's likely to be trashed unless a well-known entertainer or public figure will attend the ceremony.
6. Most editors prefer not to be called and asked, "Did you get my mail?" "Will you print the release?" "When will it appear?" Very few editors will answer these questions, and most are too busy to take such calls. You'll know if it's printed, because it's your job to monitor the media outlets that receive your news. In addition, the editor will generally contact you by mail or e-mail for more details if the story is chosen for publication.

7. Type "-30-" or "# # #" at the end of the release to indicate completion.

These rules still stand today when submitting your news by mail. However, many reporters prefer e-mail contact, which is explained later.

Press Release Dos and Don'ts

It's one thing to describe how to create a news release, but seeing the real thing provides a visual blueprint to get the media contacting you as soon as possible. You've seen one option at the beginning of the chapter. Here's another that shows how not to write a release (before), and the follow-up showing the edited version (after).

The "before" news release is similar to an advertisement, using clichés and jargon such as "cutting edge" and "business model," terms that customers won't necessarily understand. The "after" version introduces a human side to the story, which draws media attention and informs the public about the company's free skills-building workshops. The latter release also mentions that photographs are available. If you have photos of students training on-site that can be released for publication, let the media know by including this sentence directly under the contact name and phone number.

In short, look at the way good news articles are structured. You'll no doubt see that none of the stories are written in terms stating, "We're the best, the fastest, the greatest." Many stories spotlight a particular company, but other topics focus on stories that inform the reader of his or her rights and options as well as provide ideas for business or personal use. Think about this as you develop a press release. Anything submitted to an

News Release—Before

NEW COMPUTER TRAINING COMPANY TO OPEN

Technology Tigers is the name of a new, cutting-edge training facility that's opening on Tuesday, January 4. It will offer classes in word processing, spreadsheets, and how to surf the Internet.

Company president Roy Robins and trainer Sandy Smith will teach most of the classes. The company is searching for more teachers to grow the business model.

As more and more people look to learn new skills, Technology Tigers will be there to help.

The address for Technology Tigers is 125 Sugarsweet Road in Buffalo. To sign up for a class, call the company at (716) 555-6304.

###

Technology Tigers
125 Sugarsweet Road
Buffalo, NY 10836
Phone: (716) 555-6304

FOR IMMEDIATE RELEASE
Contact: Roy Robins, Day/Evening (716) 555-6304
Photographs available on request

Buffalo, NY (January 4, 2007)—Laid off from her factory job of 20 years, Beverly Taylor was scared and had to make a decision: Should she file for unemployment and hope to make ends meet, or would learning new technology skills allow her to make a rewarding career change?

Taylor, a Buffalo resident, enrolled in a free trial course at Technology Tigers. The 12-week class taught her how to create documents using word processing and data management software. Taylor now works as a freelance consultant for two firms that hire her to manage work flow.

Technology Tigers is once again offering free, trial courses throughout January as part of its New Year, New You month. Roy Robins, president, started the Buffalo-based company in January 2005 to help retrain individuals downsized from long-term jobs. "Residents need to be retrained after working for one company for so long," said Robins, who has worked in technology for 30 years. "Once our clients learn through the free trial, they come back for other training to keep their skills up to date." Technology Tigers also specializes in training staff on-site at employers' facilities.

For more information about free courses and upcoming classes, contact Robins at (716) 555-6304, or visit the Technology Tigers' Web site at www.Buffalotechtogo.com.

###

editor that's self-serving will be tossed into the garbage. Rather than writing that a product or service is "the best thing since sliced bread," explain the benefits to society, the business world, or everyday people.

Getting the Media Involved

Many businesses add another aspect to a press release that editors and reporters love: participation. Invite a reporter to be a trainee at a facility or a chocolatier for the day at a store.

Suggest that the reporter bring a camera crew to film the process on-site. That's the type of priceless publicity available when a reporter is invited to get involved. If participation is being solicited, it's wise to e-mail the reporter about the special event to ensure that the person is able to attend, placing it on his calendar as soon as possible. One week's notice is adequate. A telephone call to confirm the reporter's attendance is also acceptable.

Think about how your product or service helps the community, provides health relief benefits, gives moms a rest from the burdens of new motherhood, relaxes overworked individuals, brings joy and comfort to seniors or hospitalized patients, or educates the public about personal security. These are the angles the media yearns to print. You started a business because of a need expressed by individuals with a demand. Think about marketing with that specific angle in mind. From there you'll be able to create a news release that has the potential for local and international distribution.

What if Technology Tigers hasn't opened its doors and doesn't have a satisfied customer to quote? A free training day can still be promoted to show potential clients what they can expect when signing up for the service, and reporters can still be part of the opening day festivities. That's the hook that gets attention. For this scenario, here are the first two press release paragraphs.

Free training courses in word processing and data management will be offered throughout January at Technology Tigers as part of its New Year, New You celebration. Roy Robins, president of the Buffalo-based firm, opened the facility in January 2005 to help individuals who are unemployed.

"People need to be retrained after working for one company for decades," said Robins, who's worked in technology for 30 years. "Once our clients learn new skills through the free trial, they come back for other training to keep their skills up to date." The company also specializes in training staff on-site at most employers' facilities.

A certified public accountant (CPA) is another type of solo business owner who may be unaware of ways to create newsworthy publicity. This service provider might start by writing articles to educate readers within her specialty. If the CPA focuses on personal taxes, articles submitted to the media explaining how to choose accounting software provide a welcome story. A CPA working with corporations might turn to industry trade magazines to submit a column or story that explains new tax laws that trigger audits, which educates corporate readers and pinpoints the CPA's expertise. Other angles are available to write similar articles for different types of accounting clients. In addition, the media will publish information about free seminars to be held at libraries and other public facilities. Attorneys, veterinarians, insurance agents, and many other solo and home-based business owners benefit from this same newsworthy focus.

Every business has an angle that gets news coverage. Think about the main focus of your firm and promote that angle to its fullest potential.

Deciding Who Receives Your News

Just because you are a participant in one industry does not mean that other industries and groups are barred from receiving your press release. Many industries work together and count on each other for longevity. That makes it your duty to know about and participate in the industries and groups that depend on your information to keep them up to date on the latest trends you've uncovered.

For example, a caterer sends information about her business to trade magazines, but depending on her specialty, the caterer has many options for distributing additional news. Consider these ideas.

- Lifestyle or food sections in the newspaper get menu-planning tips.
- Senior magazines receive ideas on keeping salt or sugar content low while maintaining taste.
- Weight-loss newsletters and magazines get substitution tips to keep foods low in fat and calories while high in flavor.
- Baby magazines and Web sites receive tips to make natural foods rich in nutrients to aid babies' development.

- Party planner publications receive a list of trendsetting foods that parties are ordering for guests.

Pick and choose the ideas for promotion in the circles that gain you the most publicity. A caterer may not use every option, but this type of brainstorming uncovers the best methods to keep the caterer successfully marketing through sharing expert ideas and tips.

If your target market reads different publications, it's wise to consider all the options to keep your name in the spotlight. Customizing story ideas means you will be contacting various editors, and that's what we'll address next.

Finding Editors to Receive News

Editors are individuals who receive our news releases. They read a submission and make decisions to use it immediately, file it for future reference, or discard it. Some business owners wrongly believe that once a story is submitted, the press is obligated to print it. They're not. Consider the *New York Times'* slogan: "All the news that's fit to print." The word "fit" refers to your story's focus in relation to the newspaper, not space constraints. I've met many *New York Times* editors and have submitted news to them. To date nothing's been published, but that doesn't mean I won't continue to submit news for future publication. You may experience more immediate results in the local newspaper. That's what worked for me.

No product or service can be sold without researching the marketplace, and the same is true for finding editors and journalists to whom you submit news releases. Understanding the topics within each reporter's scope (also referred to as what they "cover") and how they craft news stories is critical to getting your information printed. You may not have time to read every article an editor publishes. That's why it's suggested that you skim articles to get a sense for how the editor selects newsworthy material. This research saves you lots of advertising money because you need not pay for ads when press release submissions gain you more promotion and sales than buying expensive advertisements.

FYI: Regional business newspapers. *Crain's*: www.crains.com. **National newspapers.** *Chicago Tribune:* www.chicagotribune.com. *Los Angeles Times:* www.latimes.com. *New York Times:* www.nytimes.com. *Wall Street Journal:* www.wsj.com. *Washington Post:* www.washington post .com. *USA Today:* www.usatoday.com. **Business magazines.** *Inc.:* www.inc.com. *Business Week:* www.businessweek.com. *Entrepreneur:* www.entrepreneur.com.

The following media sources should be at the top of your reading list:

- Local newspapers (news that affects your immediate area)
- Regional newspapers (news from other counties and surrounding towns)
- Regional business newspapers (distributed at meetings, found at selective newsstands, and sent by mail)
- National newspapers *(Chicago Tribune, Los Angeles Times, New York Times, USA Today, Wall Street Journal, Washington Post)*
- Industry trade magazines (non-newsstand publications mailed by subscription only; also found at trade shows)
- Business magazines
- General consumer magazines

Not all publications will be part of your research list. For example, local and national newspapers might bring you better coverage than a regional newspaper. Consumers may not be your focus, so that media market is omitted. You understand the target market. Searching through new media sources will prove beneficial to reach more of the target or another market segment.

Part of your research includes learning about the types of newspapers and magazines your clients read. This will help you connect with them more often as well as with others who have the potential to work with you or contract your services.

You can research and select newspapers and editors on the weekend. Go out on a Saturday or Sunday and buy all of the newspapers and magazines that could potentially receive your press releases. Then find a room in your home or office and get comfortable. Set up your laptop or use pen and paper and take plenty of notes, including:

- Newspaper names, addresses, and Web sites
- Editors and their sections
- Editors' e-mail addresses (Each section contains a reference box stating the preferred way to contact the editor.)
- Types of section features (how-to, columns, questions and answers, etc.)

You could always visit a library and capture the same information there, but you may find it wise to buy some publications rather than review borrowed copies.

Use the "News Release Distribution" chart at the end of this chapter as a guideline. The Research Date column next to the editor's name lets you record when you last checked the editor's name and title. Editors and reporters are employees. They rarely keep their jobs for life. Wherever you submit news, you must check the editor in each section every few months, updating your checklist to reflect changes. It's a mistake not to confirm that the contact person is the same each time news is sent. Quick verification keeps the lines of communication open and strengthens ties with reporters.

Fifteen Proven Tips for Great Media Relations

Getting mentioned in the news will always be an important marketing function for solo and home-based business owners. Results take planning and patience, and that's why you should not give up if one, two, or ten of your releases aren't published. Remember that you are not alone. Professional press release writers get the same nonpublished "results" as you. But many don't accept the results gracefully. During a New York press relations breakfast meeting, I was appalled to hear how editors are treated by professional press relations firms that don't get the coverage they desire. Some of the PR folks are rude by phone and leave messages in foul language for editors who do not promote an event or product launch. You cannot expect to get mentioned if you make enemies of the very people who are in line to become allies.

The editors who spoke at the breakfast work in business, consumer, and television media. They reiterated that tried-and-true marketing techniques were still the norm, and they shared tips that consistently get attention no matter where you live and work. As you move forward to find editors for getting your name in the news and building on your success, keep these fifteen techniques in mind.

1. *Focus on big issues.* Certain topics get lots of press coverage. This includes health, major holidays, the Internet, and baby boomers. Tell editors how your product or service benefits any of these markets or others that are hot topics in your area. This increases the chance for media coverage.
2. *Use e-mail to make contact.* Media contact by e-mail is better than snail mail, the telephone, and the fax. Make the subject line short and to the point. Once opened, the

message must be brief and focused, following the outline for a mailed release. Don't deliver news that mirrors a commercial! Be clear about the benefit to the reader, putting that news in the first paragraph.

3. *Double-check e-mails for misspellings.* Review your message thoroughly before clicking the Send button. Incorrect spellings, sending your message to the wrong editor, and forgetting to add your telephone number and/or Web site link won't put you on good terms with each media contact.

4. *Build relationships.* Get to know each editor's section. Consider contacting the bureau chief, another editorial person who approves stories featured in each publication. Their names can usually be found on newspaper Web sites.

5. *Become familiar with their world.* The more you know about the media and how it operates, the better your chances for coverage in print, on radio, on television, and on the Internet. This is a must to get your marketing message accepted faster.

6. *Never use a cell phone to leave a message.* When conveyed by cell phone, telephone numbers and other crucial information often become garbled or difficult to understand. The reporter will not track you down to return the call.

7. *Put patience at the top of your list.* Don't get upset if the media don't respond to your first, second, or even third news release.

There are many reasons for silence, including holding the idea until it becomes a hot topic or waiting for a reporter to return from an assignment.

8. *Plan ahead.* Newspapers and television shows may contact you quickly for an interview or feature story, but magazines work with a five- to six-month lead time. If you sell heating supplies, plan to contact a magazine editor with tips or a story idea by June, six months before the cold-weather season arrives. Keep this in mind as you schedule your releases, especially if there's a seasonal aspect to your business.

9. *Be above reproach.* Stretching the truth, telling fibs, and similar tactics are sure to be discovered, so it's best to promise only what you can deliver. One violation will make a reporter turn his back on you for good.

10. *Write envelopes by hand.* When sending information by mail, hand write the envelope. It's a personal touch and almost guarantees that the envelope will be opened more quickly than typewritten or computer-generated mail.

11. *Consider column submissions.* Newspapers and magazines feature columns that may be perfect for your story. Be sure to review column topics in case your business can be profiled in this section.

12. *Include numbers when possible.* Statistics always get media attention. Mention pertinent data within your release, and verify the

source in relation to the story idea.

13. *Avoid double pitching.* Offer your news story to one reporter at a time within the same media source. Reporters don't appreciate learning that you've been featured in different parts of a newspaper or magazine within the same issue.

14. *Prepare for evergreen topics.* Certain stories are covered every year, such as how to save money heating or cooling a home, keeping weight under control during the holidays, and gift ideas for Valentine's Day. Be ready to pitch along these lines if your company fits the category.

15. *Start a blog, and update it often.* Blogs aren't read by all reporters, but they are becoming more popular as a source for expert information. In the near future blogs may become an important research tool that gets you as much or more coverage as news releases.

Blogs are often compared to journals. When you visit a blog, the date that each entry (also known as a post) was written appears next to, above, or below the post. For home-based business owners, blogs are more than journal entries. They provide you with an opportunity to promote your expertise through written communication. There's no limit to the number of postings shared with readers, and you can post to your blog often or randomly. Creating a blog is a smart move for today's business owner.

See a sample blog at www.solobusiness marketing.com/blog/nfblog. Chapter 7 will help you get started if you don't already maintain a blog.

Follow these tips carefully. Violate them and you're sure to sabotage your media coverage. Remember, you have a vested interest in making sure your story gets printed in as many media outlets as possible. Ensure that the relationships you start are built on a strong foundation so that you can approach each media source repeatedly.

Using Editorial Calendars

Every magazine and some newspapers create an editorial calendar, a yearly schedule of approved topics that will be featured each month. Many of these calendars are posted on media Web sites; if so, such information can be beneficial in your planning. Using these calendars dovetails with tips 8 and 14 mentioned above. For example, if a magazine will feature a report on greeting cards, and you own a greeting card company, you will want to be included in that feature story. Therefore, you must contact the editor about a month before the editorial deadline shown on the publication's calendar to be considered as an information source within the story.

I monitor multiple editorial calendars during the year, contacting managing editors when I see a story that will garner publicity. The tactic works most times. The letter on the next page is an example of what I send by e-mail when contacting an editor to propose my participation.

Dear ___,

I'm Shirley Frazier, an 18-year gift and gourmet consultant and owner of Sweet Survival, a specialty marketing firm located in New Jersey. Please consider me as a contact for your upcoming report on cakes, pies, and cookies scheduled for the November issue. My clients, some of whom sell confections, receive three tips from me on maximizing their sales.

1. Piggyback on manufacturers' ad campaigns. This relationship strengthens wholesale ties while helping customers find a local source.
2. Participate in industry calendars. Costs are split between 12 or more companies, and the calendar is distributed to thousands of buyers.
3. Place your money on cause marketing. Donate a portion of sales to a charity that will promote your business in their campaign literature.

Additional information can be found on my Web site at www.solobusinessmarketing.com, or you can reach me by return e-mail or telephone at (973) 279-2799. Thank you for your consideration.

Shirley Frazier

*Adding tips within the initial introduction tells reporters that you are an expert with ideas to share and someone who will make their job easier. If you are contacted for story inclusion, be ready for an editor who's on a tight schedule. You'll receive a set of questions to be answered by phone or e-mail, whichever is best for both of you. Let the editor know when to expect your answers, and stick to your promise. The earlier you respond, the more the editor will appreciate and remember you. Once you've sent your answers, keep the questions and responses in a folder. You'll find the data to be helpful the next time an editor requests your participation.

When the article is published, request additional copies of the publication. If the article is available on the Web, be sure to attach a link to your Web site, and monitor the link for several months. As mentioned earlier, publications tend to break links without notification.

Remember to send the editor a personally written note after the article appears in print. The words "thank you" are inappropriate in the journalism world because they suggest favoritism. Do not send a gift, as that is considered a bribe. But you can still express your appreciation. Following is a sample note I've written on a personalized business note card.

Dear ___,

Tea retailers are certain to find great ideas through your recent article, and I'm pleased to have shared my insights with your readers. The article will help tea sellers increase sales by choosing the best flavors for their customers.

Contact me if I can be of assistance in the future. I'm always happy to provide tips.

Yours truly,

Shirley Frazier

Online News Release Distribution

Editors are one group that will read your press releases. Then there's another group that wants to *distribute* your news. The Internet is where you'll find many free and paid venues for online promotion at the touch of a button. The number of online distribution services seems to grow every day, but the real question is whether or not to include them in your plan. Will these services net you better, adequate, or insignificant results compared to contacting editors directly?

An online news release distribution service is a Web-based outlet that assists large and small businesses, in all industries, gain media attention to promote new products, services, and newsworthy events on a no-fee basis or for a nominal cost. These services accept press releases from businesses with a legitimate marketing agenda. In other words, Web sites selling pornographic products and illegal services are not accepted for press distribution. Those types of services don't

seem to need promotion. It's the rest of us who require help.

Free Distribution Options

When I first became aware of Web-based press release services that spread news to media outlets around the world at no cost to me, I had only one question: What's in it for them? One answer is that these distribution services encourage you to pay for additional press distribution over and above that provided through the free option. But the reason is not important. The services exist for your use, free or otherwise.

You can find numerous distribution services through Internet search engines. You'll be required to subscribe to each service, creating a user name and password to access your account. Create a bookmark in your Internet Favorites folder called "press releases" or another memorable name. This bookmark, which is accessible through you Internet browser (Internet Explorer,

Firefox, Netscape, etc.), saves the Web site's address so that at the click of a mouse, you easily return to each press release submission page.

Each distributor requires specific information when submitting your news release. This information helps distribute your news to the right media sources in the most expeditious way. You'll be asked for:

A submission date. Distribution services provide you with guidelines as to what submission date is permissible. A date two days ahead of time is normal. For example, if today is June 1, a generally accepted submission date is June 3 or later.

An article summary. What's the basis for your news? The summary is often captured in the first paragraph. It's okay to use the first two sentences of a release as a summary as long as it capsulizes the release.

A distribution category and subcategory. This is a breakdown of the industry to which you belong and any subtopic for the featured release. For example, if you own a pet products company, the category may be "retail" or "pets" or "animals," with a subcategory of "accessories." Subcategories aren't always required. Look at the long list of categories before making your choice.

Main keywords. Create a list of words from the release that best describe its content. This will help reporters who are looking for certain topics find them through keyword selection.

After creating your account subscriptions, follow this blueprint to submit your news.

1. Write your news release. Use the information explained in this chapter to develop one release for distribution.
2. Sign in to each Web account, and complete the submission form. Double-check your work to make sure each area is complete.
3. Once the release is submitted, you will receive a document number from most distribution outlets. This number will let you monitor the release's processing and final publication.
4. Add each news release link to your own Web site for easy access by anyone looking for the latest information about your business or industry. Your online media room is the best place to feature the news release link. (See chapter 5 for more on media rooms.)

Service Upgrades

You'll notice that distribution services offer added options at a cost. While free options bring you limited publicity, paying for expanded distribution can put your news into the hands of reporters who regularly depend on releases featured on Yahoo.com, CNNMoney.com, Google.com, and other well-known sources.

It's unclear why most, if not all, free releases aren't featured through the popular news sites. However, part of your plan may include investing less than $100 to upgrade a release you wish to distribute in wider circles. Depending on the industry, topic, and keywords used, you may find that paying for upgraded service gets your news featured on the popular Internet news sites as well as in print publications.

Conduct research to determine if the service upgrade is worthwhile. This includes visiting online message boards and blogs to ask participants about their experience. Review each distribution service's investment costs and the news outlets that are promised to receive your release. Create a checklist to document your findings, and choose the site that gives you the best distribution for the money.

Results will vary whether you select the free or paid option. Solo owners have found success in both cases. Timeliness and your chosen industry affect media coverage, which is why the outcome differs from person to person. If you have a terrific message to broadcast and can afford the low investment, move forward without hesitation.

Paid Distribution Options

Some services operate on a fee-only distribution basis. That's because they are at the top of the distribution chain. These outlets are the best sources on and off the Web for press release delivery not only because they've existed for years, before the Web became the great tool it is, but also because they work hand in hand with the media sources we know best. This includes the *New York Times*, CNN, and regional newspapers that provide wide coverage in areas that are otherwise difficult to reach.

PRNewswire: www.prnewswire.com. Market Wire: www.marketwire.com.

In many cases paid services are news bureaus that send your release directly to the editor in charge of the section that covers your particular industry. If you believe that sending your news through this source is a wise decision, in place of or in addition to direct contact with reporters by mail or e-mail, then this strategy is one to try.

When you visit the paid news distribution sites, you'll notice that they guarantee distribution in the regions you specify. Your news release will be delivered, but just like news sent through the less-expensive option, it may or may not be published, so results also vary here even though you pay. The wider the distribution, the more you pay, and the costs are expensive for most solo and home-based business owners. Still, the chance of seeing your name in the news are more likely with the paid distribution services than with the free ones. This is one area where "you get what you pay for" still applies.

The options for media coverage can overwhelm a busy business owner. The urge to take advantage of each option is powerful, but putting every task on your list is not a smart decision, especially at the beginning. Brainstorm the possibilities, select the best course of action, and publish your news releases each month to increase media exposure and the publicity you deserve throughout the year.

News Release Distribution Worksheet

MEDIA SOURCE	MEDIA NAME	SECTION/FEATURES	EDITOR	
	Address/Web Site	(how-to, Q&A, etc.)	Name/E-mail	Date of Research
Newspapers				
Local				
Regional				
National				
International				
Magazines				
State				
Industry (trade)				
Specialty (food, etc.)				
Trade				
Newspapers				
Magazines				
Web Distribution				
Free				
Paid				

05

Making Yourself a Broadcast Media Darling

If you're eager to get up close and personal with potential buyers by way of radio, television, and cable, this is the chapter to read to learn all about getting your fifteen minutes of fame. In television terms that's five three-minute segments, each of which seems like a lifetime during a live broadcast! The payback can be enormous, and so can the preparation if you sell a product to be demonstrated on the air or offer a service in a tight niche. But where else can you find an audience of that magnitude, no matter what the medium?

Niche marketing definition. http://en.wikipedia.org/wiki/Niche _marketing.

Why the Broadcast Media Want You

The concept of a show—whether on television, cable, or radio—is to provide programming of interest to the target audience. Each show is manned by at least one producer, and his responsibility is to find guests who bring ideas and insights to viewers or listeners. That means every year thousands of people will be invited to share their message. One of those thousands should be you.

Why do the media search for people to fill broadcasts? Airtime costs money, and the media seek advertising dollars from companies with deep pockets to pay for broadcasts. While you hope to make a splash on the air, your segment is generating thousands of dollars for the station.

Which media markets are best? Many broadcasts are available to host your appearance, but only the shows that match your unique message are the best to make your short list of candidates. There are other considerations to ensure that you select the right media sources to promote what you sell.

- Is a visual or spoken message best? Products are better demonstrated on television and cable, while someone offering a service can use either radio or TV as a sales tool.
- What does the target audience prefer? If buyers listen to radio during the morning commute, it may be wise to approach radio shows.
- Should you focus on local or national promotion? Knowing where the most likely buyers are located helps you to decide if local stations are the first priority or if going after shows with national distribution is the best approach.

Should You Seek Help to Get Broadcasting Publicity?

Outsourcing the job of finding publicity is worth consideration. Professional media relations specialists, known as publicists, work with and have access to show producers and other important contacts in broadcasting. Publicists exist to help clients find media segments, taking the work out of your hands so you can concentrate on other projects. A publicist provides a smooth transition to get your face and/or voice into millions of households, cars, and offices around the world.

But this help comes at a price—from several hundred to several thousand dollars. If you want to work with a publicist, you'll have to decide if the cost makes sense compared to the expected return. Review the publicist's track record and get that record verified by the publicist's past clients. Ask for details of real benefits received through the alliance.

Like anything else in business, a publicist cannot guarantee results. She looks at what you have to offer, decides which avenues to take to proceed with media contact, and moves forward to pitch your expertise by e-mail, regular mail, or telephone. Many solo and home-based entrepreneurs act as their own publicist because their budgets don't allow them to hire one. Publicity is another part of the marketing puzzle that's achievable if you're ready for broadcast fame.

A Do-It-Yourself Primer

Your Public Best: The Complete Guide to Making Successful Public Appearances in the Meeting Room, on the Platform, and on TV, by Lillian Brown, was my bible for finding and preparing for my first television appearances. At the time the book was five years old, yet even by today's standards it is relevant. The book contains these smart facts:

- Contact the show's producer, not the on-air personality.
- Find producers' names in media books found in the library's reference section.
- Wear a color other than white, especially

Potential Media Sources Worksheet

Media Type/Show Name	Location (Address, Phone, Web)	Audience (Local, etc.)	Producer's Name/Phone/E-mail	Date of Contact/ Comments
TELEVISION				
CABLE				
RADIO				
SATELLITE				

on the upper torso, when appearing on television.

- Sell the producer on the informational benefits or expertise you'll share with the audience rather than the actual product or service.
- Ask if makeup will be applied at the television or cable studio. If not, be ready to take the shine off your own nose.
- If makeup will be provided at the studio, look up when eyeliner is being applied. Otherwise close your eyes when your face is "under construction."

Now let's incorporate those tips into a broadcast-savvy publicity plan that will get you fame and thousands of dollars in sales.

1. *Make a list of all media outlets available to you.* That includes television, cable, and radio stations. This is done by researching broadcasters in your local television and radio area that welcome guest appearances. Look for show producers' names on media Web sites. Names won't appear on the home page, so be ready to drill down through levels of pages to find the right contacts. Sure, this is a lot of work, but it's worth your time if you want to appear or be heard on a particular show.

Keep in mind that there are many more stations available that are not in your area. Regional shows are good starters, but consider the bigger picture. Look for shows with mass appeal that reach smaller, targeted markets.

Consult the *Gale Directory of Publications and Broadcast Media* in your local library. This massive reference book lists media sources you may not have considered, complete with contact names, titles, telephone numbers, and e-mail addresses. Bring your pad and pen or notebook computer to document your findings, or make copies of the Potential Media Sources Worksheet and fill it in as you go.

With list of markets in hand, decide which broadcast type is the best outlet for your product or service. This decision depends in part on whether your product needs to be seen or if radio will work to spread your message.

2. *Create a press or media room on your Web site* to provide general information about your business and specific insights on your expertise. Many Web sites contain media rooms, so don't reinvent the wheel in deciding what type of information to include in your own media room. If you type the words "press room" or "media room" into a search engine, you'll find thousands of pages belonging to businesses in all industries. Ideally look for media rooms that belong to competitors and related professions. This will give you a good start as you put your page together. Over time you can add more material to your press

room. More details about what to include is discussed later in this chapter.

3. *Create a compelling statement explaining the product's or service's benefit to viewers and/or listeners.* Match your marketing to seasons, upcoming events, and current trends to make your appearance a timely benefit. Write this marketing script, also known as a pitch, on paper so you know exactly what to say when the producer picks up the phone. Writing your script ahead of time ensures that you don't fumble over words. Practice your pitch several times before calling to make sure your voice is smooth and confident. (Read the case study sidebar for an idea of what to include in a successful pitch.)

4. *Send follow-up information in the requested format.* Such materials include a letter of introduction, product sheets, interview clippings, and letters from satisfied clients. Be ready to send these marketing materials by express mail, if requested. It's a small investment to get the publicity you deserve. In most cases you won't have to send information by mail, since many producers prefer the immediacy of e-mail over mail or fax. Ask each contact if e-mail attachments are acceptable or if another format is preferred. Then send the details as quickly as possible.

Getting your first big break on television or radio is a thrill. Soon after that you begin looking

CASE STUDY: MY FIRST TASTE OF TELEVISION

In the mid-1990s I designed gift baskets, a product best shared with audiences through television. I studied different shows, watching each segment to determine where I might fit in. I consulted library books to learn about target markets and to find other shows that would benefit my business.

The first show on my list, hosted by Robin Leach, aired at 10:00 p.m. on the Food Network. White-collar workers ages twenty-five to forty-nine and living in the New York metropolitan area were the target. I believed these viewers wanted to see my product. My mission was to speak with the producer and convince him to let me appear.

I had learned that if you cannot find the producer's name ahead of time, the best course of action is to call the studio and ask to speak with the show producer. That's what I did. Armed with a script that explained the benefits viewers would receive from my appearance, I called the Food Network and asked to speak with the show's producer. The phone rang, and a gentleman answered.

"Dwayne King."

"Hello, I'm Shirley Frazier. I'm a big fan of [show name], and I'm also a gift consultant. Summer will...."

"Hi, Shirley!"

Without thinking, I pulled the phone from my ear and glanced at it. I thought, "I'm calling New York. Who gives you a warm and cozy feeling during the first conversation?" I quickly squished the receiver back to my ear.

"Hi, Dwayne! Summer will arrive next week, and I'd love to show your audience how to create picnics for two in the comfort of their home. If you're interested I'll send you some photos and other details to see if it's right for the show."

"That sounds great. Send it to me, and I'll take a look."

I quickly wrote Dwayne's full name and address and started thinking about what to send him. A glossy black folder with inside pockets on either side looked attractive. I began gathering materials to fill the folder: my letter of introduction, business card, newspaper press clippings, picnic basket photographs, a list of individual and corporate client names, and copies of appreciation letters.

I attached a label with my business name and telephone number to the front of the folder. The package was complete, but it seemed lifeless. Something was missing, something that would dazzle Dwayne and influence him to put me on the show. I thought about Robin Leach and what to include in the package specifically for him. Because Robin is originally from the United Kingdom, tea and cake came to mind. I searched my gift basket inventory and found an English teacup and saucer and Earl Grey tea. I packaged freshly baked shortbread cookies and then wrapped the cookies, tea, cup, and saucer together with cellophane and topped the gift with a bow. The gift and folder were placed in a glossy black bag with cord handles. Everything was ready for presentation.

The package was too important to entrust to postal handlers, so I decided to deliver it by hand. I called my mother and asked her to accompany me to New York. We were on our way in less than an hour.

The two of us and the package sailed through the Lincoln Tunnel in record time. Two trucks were parked in front of the Food Network building with enough space between them to tuck my Dodge Caravan. The delivery plan was working.

My mom remained in the car, poised to drive around the block if she was told to move the vehicle. I entered the building, excited and breathless. One of the security officers gave me an entrance pass and I was on my way to the thirty-first floor.

Dwayne wasn't expecting me, so I left the package with a Food Network receptionist. I left the building moments later. The forty-mile round-trip excursion and delivery took just forty-five minutes.

An hour later I received a call from Dwayne. He loved the package and promised to try and book me on the show. Dwayne and I traded phone calls all summer. I never appeared on the show, but Dwayne shared my folder with another producer with whom I secured a relationship. My persistence paid off with numerous guest appearances on another Food Network show, which produced lots of publicity and many sales.

at your publicity efforts very critically, focusing your energy on marketing to audiences who are ready to buy from you. Everyone wants to appear on national television and cable shows, as well as those radio stations with hundreds of affiliates, but will you get as many sales from them as you do from local markets? That's what you test and research, and then you make your decision based on what's best in terms of time and monetary potential.

Satellite Radio

Your opportunities to be featured on radio have expanded thanks to satellite programming. Local stations are your first priority. Beyond that, your radio marketing research should include XM and Sirius, the two competing national satellite stations presently considering a merger. Both are growing by leaps and bounds in subscribers and in talk show segments.

XM Radio: www.xmradio.com. Sirius: www.sirius.com.

Just as you watched television and cable shows to locate broadcast markets, so must you listen to satellite radio. Subscribing to satellite radio at about $12 per month for each station, not counting the receiver price and other accessories, may be more than your budget can handle. In that case, look for free trial offers. Both XM and Sirius, for example, offer a downloadable, free

Shirley Says

A WORD ABOUT GIFTS

In today's post–September 11 security-conscious world, I suggest that only informational documents be given to producers rather than gifts of any kind. Buying products becomes costly, and it doesn't guarantee an appearance. In fact, gift giving at the beginning of a business relationship or after the segment concludes can be seen as inappropriate. It can appear to some as preferential treatment toward the person who presents the biggest or most-expensive gift. Many broadcasters frown on gifts, no matter what you've heard or read in the press.

trial on the Internet. The free option may not give you access to every channel, but you can view each service's channel lineup on its respective Web site. You'll see what segments may fit your marketing campaign. If you've had success contacting television show producers, you can use the same approach with satellite and traditional radio stations.

Tell everyone about your desire to be a guest on television, cable, radio, and satellite programs. Spreading the word has the potential to uncover sources and insiders whom you didn't know, and great discoveries usually occur in your own backyard. For example, a neighbor's brother may be affiliated with a radio station, or a church deacon might work for a major cable network. It's smart to use word of mouth to broaden the marketing potential.

If you do not know of or cannot find anyone to help, do what you do best—use your ingenuity. That includes areas covered in this chapter:

- E-mailing or calling show or segment producers.
- Using library books to uncover broadcast stations.
- Delivering a marketing package to a show producer.
- Creating an online media room.
- Downloading satellite radio and listening to broadcasts that match your marketing needs.

Broadcasts—Live or Taped?

Preparing for media marketing opportunities consists of being ready for *every* type of broadcast. It's almost guaranteed that a radio station segment will be live, but television and cable work as live *or* taped transmissions, depending on the show's format. Morning television shows are usually live, but shows aired on stations such as Home & Garden Television (HGTV) and Lifetime are usually taped.

The live television format is quick, with no retakes or rehearsals. You are asked to arrive at the studio at a specific time, usually one to two hours in advance, to ensure you are on the premises and ready for the appearance. You and other guests gather in the "green room," a comfortable space that accommodates visitors before and after broadcast appearances. At a major network or its affiliate, this room will have chairs, tables, beverages, and snacks. Most guests do not eat before airing to ensure that their breath stays fresh. You, too, should refrain from eating.

FYI: Green room facts. http://en.wikipedia.org/wiki/Green_room.

When it's time for your appearance, you are escorted into the studio. A technician attaches a microphone to your lapel or collar. The show's host greets you and quickly interacts with you about the segment. You'll hear a countdown, which alerts everyone in the studio to the number of minutes or seconds before the show is live. When the countdown reduces to 3, 2, 1—smile—and get ready to tell the world about your product or service. Everyone wants to hear why you're appearing on the show and how it benefits them.

One part of the producer's media package that wasn't mentioned earlier is the ten-question script that guides the host during the segment. You prepare these ten questions, which are designed to share with the audience a mix of basic knowledge about your specialty and some little-known facts. But be warned. Few, if any, of the questions will be part of the broadcast. Hosts won't ask embarrassing or prying questions, but they might ask about a part of the business that you hadn't considered.

Think about your responses before answering to lessen the ums, aahs, and "you know" phrases that are heard when guests fumble to find the right words. Such phrases are usually a sign of nervousness, which is common during the first few appearances. Don't fret if this happens to you. As with every experience, you'll learn what to do and how to combat the anxiety. Take a few breaths and, most of all, stay levelheaded. The more you envision the broadcast as a casual conversation between you and the host, the more relaxed you become, and the best ideas and information will flow naturally.

This television and cable scenario applies to radio, the only major difference being that your voice is the selling tool on the airwaves. And instead of taping from the station, you may be asked to call in. The producer will ask you for contact information to share with the audience. This will be your toll-free or general telephone number, Web site address, or other details that relate to the reason you're on the air.

Live television segments last between three to six minutes, while radio time depends on the show's format. When your segment concludes, you either return to the green room to satisfy your sudden hunger or leave the studio.

A taped television format takes longer to complete than a live segment, but the benefit is that the segment will play several times during a season, and it may be rebroadcast at other times in the year. Each person who appears on a taped show is given a certain time slot for taping. They are groomed, the area within the studio is prepared for their segment, and then taping begins. It can take several hours to finalize one person's segment. That means if you are one of three people to be taped that day, there's a chance that you'll be in the studio all day, especially if you're last on the list. Take advantage of the time by watching what goes on in front and in back of the camera.

Talk with studio personnel, if possible, about other opportunities to appear on shows at that facility and similar places. Distribute and collect studio personnel business cards, and stay in contact with these folks. The connections you make here can go a long way toward landing future appearances on shows across the country.

One person in particular with great insights is the makeup artist. She is privy to lots of information that you won't learn from studio executives, such as what perks to request when you'll be in the studio all day. These perks include travel expense coverage and a free stay at a nearby hotel the night before or after taping.

While you are in the studio, it is acceptable to ask the producer for a segment tape. If taping is live, you'll receive the video before you leave or later by mail. If your segment is taped and edited before being shown on television, it can take several months to receive a tape. You want this tape to critique your appearance and responses, as well as to share with other parties who may consider you for upcoming shows and nonbroadcast speaking engagements.

After-Show Follow-up

Put your follow-up plan in motion before you leave the studio. Here's what to do.

1. Ask the producer for his card. Make sure his e-mail address is included, and ask if it's appropriate to make contact by e-mail or if another method is preferred.

2. Ask the producer when you can contact him again for another appearance. The timing will depend on what you sell, seasonal trends, and current events.

3. Contact the producer about two weeks after the show's airing. Give him figures on the responses you've received. This includes the number of people who contact you by telephone, e-mail, fax, and regular mail. Include the number of sales transacted due to your appearance. This information establishes your popularity and supports the reason to book a return visit.

4. Follow up to secure another appearance, as dictated by the time schedule set in step 2 above.

5. Ask the producer for the names of other show producers within that network if another show seems to be a good match to market your product or service.

6. Contact the producer when there's something of interest to ask or share. Do not e-mail him excessively or you will be labeled a pest and will not be given another opportunity to appear on that network.

There is another follow-up component that solo business owners should monitor, and that is *results*. Now that you've presented yourself on air, think about the work it took to get you on television or radio as well as the time invested to make this dream come true. Was it everything you hoped it would be? Did you receive inquiries from viewers? And the final question: Is preparing for and appearing on television or radio worth the time and effort?

Inquiries, opportunities, and sales are what some home-based business owners experience each time they appear on a broadcast. For them such segments are gravy. But for others—specifically those who must transport lots of products in their vehicle, into a studio, and then back to the office—the process is either worth the effort or a waste of time. Weigh your options each time you consider an appearance. Broadcast segments are golden opportunities. You may be asked to be part of a broadcast every four to six months, depending on the topic and industry, but you must consider the bigger picture. As long as you

are reaping benefits, television and radio are worth your time. If not, other marketing tools are at your disposal.

Do not expect overnight riches from your appearance. It will not happen. Television and radio shows receive millions of dollars in revenue from the advertisers who sponsor the shows. In turn, the broadcasters have a responsibility to find suitable guests who will feed the viewers' minds and keep advertisers happy. You also have a responsibility, which is to find the best broadcast to market your product and service to increase your store traffic, Web site visitors, and revenue. Keep focused on your own marketing plan to turn each appearance into an advantage.

06

Technological Tools and More That Maximize Marketing

Independent business owners understand the difference between creating a new wheel and reinventing the current model. Most often we look for methods to mold the standard wheel into a version that works best to sell our products and services.

One way we can create a marketing path is to look at the campaigns of large and small companies. We decide what part of those campaigns are good strategies to target our customers. Then we search for tools within our budget to launch the promotions. Finally we create the product, distribute it in several formats, and track results. If the campaign was successful, we repeat the process when the time is right.

No matter what your profession, there are certain products that will always be affordable for you to create and clients to buy. These products are helpful on their own, or they are packaged as part of your service. Chapter 1 unveiled techniques to craft your marketing plan. This chapter shows how to develop ancillary products that complement the plan.

Here's an example. I recorded a fifty-five-minute cassette tape telling aspiring entrepreneurs about the pros and cons of starting a business. The tape sells for $15. I added a $10 coupon with each sale to encourage buyers to order other products. I believed the tape would be beneficial to introduce people to my business and provide a comfort zone that encouraged them to buy more from me.

The tape's format changed from cassette to CD when disks became more popular. I also lowered the cost by $5 to attract more buyers. This product continues to sell well because listeners can hear the message while walking, driving, or exercising. A friend of mine called the tape "mobile motivation," a phrase I added to my marketing message. The product continues to be a win-win situation for buyers and me.

Whether you're just starting your business or are a seasoned professional, there are informational products you can create to enhance your marketing campaign. These include:

- Teleseminars
- Topic-based interviews
- CDs and DVDs
- Directories
- Special reports
- Web videos
- Podcasts
- Web site FAQs
- How-to guides

Let's review five marketing products that you can afford and easily fit into your campaign.

Teleseminars

Consider this: You meet another expert in your industry whose name is instantly recognizable, or perhaps this person's insights are so profound that you're compelled to stay in touch with him. You ask him to be a guest on an interview you will conduct by telephone.

Your mission is to elevate both your name recognition and his through this teleseminar, which can be heard live by telephone participants and heard later by individuals who purchase the taped conversation. Those who hear the conver-

sation live are asked to pay a small fee, and individuals who visit your Web site can purchase the tape when it's available.

Teleseminars are phone-based conversations between two or more people that educate listeners about a particular subject. Why should you add this product to your marketing? Because it's 1) easy to create, 2) affordable, 3) a way to elevate your industry status, and 4) a moneymaker as long as it's marketed on and off the Web as part of your existing products and services.

Interviewing another person is just one example of a teleseminar. Here are two more.

- You become the interviewee, which turns the spotlight on your expertise. This may be a better option than the first, but there's a catch. You must find a person who's adept at interviewing, which entails keeping the conversation interesting and on topic.
- You form a partnership with another person, and both of you present your information or views. This collaborative model keeps the content lively, no matter which topic or industry is discussed.

Teleseminars are also part "mobile motivation" because they're easy to listen to while traveling.

I've teamed up with friends and colleagues to create teleseminars that discuss sales, marketing, organizing, and small-business law. The information is evergreen and sold in CD format at seminars I conduct nationwide. The CDs are duplicated on my computer, labeled by means of custom software purchased at an office supply retailer, and packaged in CD holders purchased from wholesale or retail sources, depending on availability and cost. A popular price for these CDs is $29.95, but the price is adjusted higher or lower depending on the industry, subject matter, and any discount applied for multiple copies or orders placed during an event.

There are three methods to market and sell teleseminars:

1. Charge a fee to listeners who call in to participate in the live broadcast. An average charge is between $19 and $29. Incentives are frequently offered to generate interest, such as a free report to download when they enroll.

   Because many teleseminars are available free of charge, you may decide to offer your first event at no cost. Depending on the subject matter and industry, however, you may be able to charge a fee for participation. Research how other companies within your field, if any, conduct seminars by phone. Do they believe the information is worth buying? If so, charge a fee. If not, you can still move forward to record and sell your information.

2. Record and sell the teleseminar. The company you contract to tape the event also makes numerous phone lines available if you allow listeners to be part of the call. You will receive a master copy of the event for anyone who didn't attend the live broadcast but wants to hear about the topic.

3. Make the teleseminar transcript available by mail or e-mail for anyone who wants a text copy. Some people prefer text over tape. The script is another product sold alongside the CD.

   Once you finalize your teleseminar, you'll ask yourself why it took so long to start. You'll appreciate its simplicity and begin searching for new participants in collaborations and interviews. Best of all, you'll steadily build a network of followers who look forward to buying teleseminars.

Teleseminar Preparations

Here are the steps to holding and marketing your teleseminar.

1. *Decide on the topic.* Start with something easy. Subjects can be as simple as "Ten Ways to Safely Whiten Your Teeth" or "Twelve Tips to Find a Safe, Affordable Day Care Center." The number of tips (five, ten, fifteen, etc.) isn't important. What matters is that listeners believe they're investing their money in exchange for a fair amount of information.

2. *Choose the format.* Is it better for you to conduct the interview or have someone ask you questions? Do you want to be considered the expert, or is it better to be viewed as an expert interviewer? Do you want to share the spotlight or be seen as the star? Two people are the minimum participants

for an event, no matter which format is chosen. A one-person monologue is uninteresting. Once you decide on the format, you can create the teleseminar's structure.

3. *Invite another person to participate.* Once she agrees to be interviewed, brief her about the subject matter, how long you believe the teleseminar will run (thirty minutes to one hour is standard), and the proposed date for preparation and taping. This will ensure open communication to keep both of you on track.

4. *Write a script.* How wonderful it would be if both of you could talk for an hour, maintaining focus and clarity about the subject, with no pauses and few mistakes. That won't happen unless a script is prepared in advance. A script ensures that the participants stay focused and the teleseminar contains only the most-valuable details. It also minimizes the number of "ums" and "aahs," two pause words that no one wants to hear recorded. Pauses aren't written into copy, so few, if any, will be heard on tape.

Extemporaneous discussions not in the script are a refreshing addition. The host and guest are encouraged to share stories that complement the subject and play on each other's chemistry, especially if a point within the script reminds you of relevant facts you wish to share with listeners.

Writing a script is the most time-consuming process for this project. A good script consists of questions and answers or information to be shared by both parties. Breaks within the text indicate when one person stops talking and the other starts. A script also includes a minimum of two breaks, one at midpoint and another at the end. It's the point where "commercials" are added, informing the listener about your respective expertise, Web site URLs, and telephone numbers (phone numbers aren't needed if Web site addresses are provided). When the script is complete, it is reviewed by both parties and edited if needed. The taping can now proceed.

5. *Find and select a teleseminar recording company.* These firms are plentiful and easily found on the Web. You're looking for one that's reliable, affordable, and able to supply enough phone lines for participants. Questions to ask the recording company are:

- What is the recording charge? Is the charge dependent on length of taping time or number of lines secured for listeners?
- How long will it take, after the recording, to send a master copy by mail?
- How long do you keep a copy of the recording in case I need a duplicate because my copy was lost or damaged?
- What is the procedure if something happens during taping that makes us stop the transmission (dead phone, power outage, etc.)?

- What if I'm not satisfied with the sound or clarity? Do I have to pay for another session?

6. *Set a taping date and time.* Secure a date a month in advance if you plan to invite participants, whether they pay or listen free of charge. It's easier selecting a date when just you and the other party will tape with no audience. Simply set a date that agrees with both of you, call or e-mail the recording company to set the schedule, and confirm it with all parties the day before taping.

   If participants are invited, post details about the event on your Web site, and employ other promotional methods shared throughout this book. This includes an alert in your e-mail signature and online newsletter, notification on message boards, mailing postcards, and using word of mouth at events and meetings.

7. *Call the telephone number given to you by the recording company at least five minutes before taping.* Have water and mints nearby. Turn off your phone's call-waiting features. Use a land line (corded) phone rather than a cellular phone. Cell phones are unstable and may lose power or garble words during the session. You will be very unhappy if you must reschedule taping because of cell phone problems.

   When the recording is complete, the host company will mail you a master copy on CD.

Shirley Says

Telephone or Headphone?

My recording experience has shown that using the phone's receiver instead of a headphone attachment provides better clarity. A hissing sound is transmitted through a headphone's microphone, which is distracting during playback. The recording company may or may not be able to remove the hissing. This problem may not be associated with all headphones, but be aware in case it occurs during your taping.

Your script ensures that the content is correct. However, you must listen to the entire teleseminar to make sure it is acceptable for distribution. The recording company should be contacted immediately if there is a technical problem. Many companies will try to clean up problems in their studio, or they will let you to rerecord the content at no charge. Remember to ask if this is allowable before agreeing to the service.

8. *Market the teleseminar using a prelaunch price.* As mentioned earlier, a popular CD price is $29.95, but your price may be different due to topic structure or technicalities. As soon as the recording ends, you can encourage early sales by selling the teleseminar at a slightly lower price than what will be charged after the prelaunch period. As an added buying incentive, a free report or another product may be included to presell as many copies as possible. This is a great way to market and receive revenue in advance. It also helps to determine the subject's popularity.

9. *Listen to the recording* when the teleseminar arrives. Be excited, not fearful, of hearing your voice and the chemistry between you and the collaborator. Remember that you are an expert with a message to share with people who want to hear your ideas, words, and advice.

FYI: Definition of target market. www.marketing power.com/mg-dictionary-view3141.php.

10. *Send news releases* about the teleseminar's contents (refer to chapter 4), and add the information to all marketing materials. These materials feature details about the seminar's contents and why the conversation benefits listeners. The topic you've committed to tape is timely, trendsetting, and important to the people who want to know about the subject. Your goal is to tell everyone within the target market that your teleseminar exists.

Marketing materials encourage sales by sharing the teleseminar's highlights. Here's the partial text for a marketing teleseminar I recorded with a colleague:

> Hear this lively fifty-minute CD covering six months of savvy marketing techniques. You'll learn:
>
> - When and where to create special occasion promotions.
> - How to capitalize on little-known events that generate sales.
> - Why ethnic occasions are important and which ones to promote.
> - How pet gifts keep your sales from "pawsing."
> - Which products and services encourage year-round loyalty.
> - Where to sell products and services to "captive" audiences.

Information extracted from the teleseminar to use as a marketing tool answers the question, "What's in it for me to buy this product?" Answering that one question captures early orders and continuous sales.

Recording Costs and Projected Revenues

Taping a teleseminar costs $25 or more, depending on the recording company. The final product's retail cost is a minimum of $29.95 after the prelaunch price. The concept's low price not only creates a powerful revenue generator but also markets your expertise in two formats—in text (transcript) and teleseminar format (CD). Hundreds of both products generate sales all year as long as you continue to market. Don't be surprised if competitors begin offering this product to their customers. Just make sure that you continue to collaborate with experts who understand the potential and revenue associated with this powerful marketing product.

If duplicating the teleseminar on your computer is not possible, CD duplicating companies will perform the work. Some companies offer first-time specials, while others will duplicate a minimum of 1,000 at a time. These companies will also label and package the teleseminar, leaving you with time to find new ways to sell and create teleseminar subjects that spin into gold.

Directories

Individuals, groups, and corporations require many types of information. Some is available in books, and other forms are found on the Internet. People search for compilations created by resourceful firms because they are not in the position to gather the details on their own. Information seekers want one concise booklet or report that saves them time and energy. This is why directories on every conceivable subject are popular products that solo business owners organize and sell.

Think about this: You receive calls and e-mails every day asking for industry information. You've been referring other companies' products and services for months with no referral fee if a sale is transacted. The only way for you to profit from your knowledge is to create reference materials that list the types of resources callers request most. Such materials will turn your knowledge into a marketable product.

Here's a sample of information often requested by phone:

- Wholesalers of specific resources
- Statistics for niche industries
- Distributors of wholesale or retail services
- Resource listings for hard-to-find products

- Products or services located in specific states or regions

Directories are quick to compile and update on a yearly basis, especially when you participate in the industry that gives you access to the data. Also consider selling the product in different formats, such as:

- Text by mail
- CD by mail
- Text by e-mail
- PDF by e-mail

Because of their simplicity, directories seem to be an underappreciated product in terms of creation, but they are a valuable commodity in all industries. In some cases you will have to perform additional research to complete a directory. But your insider knowledge makes the data simple to find.

My first directory was a listing of gift industry shows throughout the United States. I created it because of the daily telephone calls and e-mails I received asking me for this material. Each interruption cost time, usually ten to twenty minutes. I realized the monetary potential and created a directory listing all industry shows. Thousands were sold for $29.95 in text format. Now that a computerized version is available, I sell many more.

Deciding Which Directories to Create

The best directories are the ones that are simple to create yet difficult for people or groups outside of your industry to compile on their own. Groups include the media, organizations that require specialized products or services, and individuals who are new to your industry.

As you start the process, consider the details you are asked to provide when callers use your company as their personal "411" service. That's the information to begin compiling. Most requests are for the following:

- Business name
- Address
- Toll-free number
- Regular telephone and fax numbers
- Web site URL and e-mail address
- Brief product or service description

  It can also include:

- Contact name
- Credit cards accepted
- Minimum order quantity or minimum dollar amount for purchases
- Other details that are basic to the industry

Directories display source information in a manner that's easy to understand. This is how a listing might be created for one type of directory.

The ABC Company	V	☑	Minimum Order: $100
123 Main Drive	MC	☑	
Buffalo, NY 15259	AX	☑	
Toll-free: (800) 555-1212	DISC	☑	
Fax: (800) 555-1213			
www.abccomp.com			Bags, ribbon, and more

Here's similar information compiled in another format for a second directory.

The ABC Company
123 Main Drive
Buffalo, NY 15259
Toll-free: (800) 555-1212
Fax: (800) 555-1213
www.abccomp.com
Bags, ribbon, and more

In the first example, the directory shows a structure arranged in a space-saving two- or three-column format. The second example allows the right side of the page to remain blank for note taking.

Not all customers want every detail about companies within your industry. Some directories require the long version, while others provide a quick sketch of industry information. Clients' questions will help you put the best-selling formats together.

Directories elevate your status as an expert because industry compilations are often created by insiders who collect this information for their own use. Because these details are important to you and contained in a Rolodex, electronic organizer, or binder, the idea occurs that the same information may be beneficial to others. Your insider knowledge turns information you consult on a daily basis into a marketable product.

Web Videos

Creating a video about your product or service, then posting and promoting it on your Web site or popular video-sharing community, is easier than you imagine. There are two ways to produce videos. One choice teams Windows Media Player with Photo Story 3. The other alternative is to purchase equipment, such as a Web camera (also known as a webcam) or camcorder, to make your videos.

Windows Media Player and Photo Story 3

This combination allows you to develop a video in storyboard format. Photos are placed in a specific format, and your voice narrates each scene to create a video. The cost to develop this type of video is measured in time because Windows Media Player and Photo Story 3 are both available free of charge through the Microsoft.com Web site. Once the video is completed, you can promote it in many ways: 1) Add a link to it in your e-mail signature, 2) put it on a CD to use as a prospecting tool, 3) show it in a client's office as a sales tool, 4) add it to your Web site for visitors to view, 5) give it away as a bonus product, or 6) sell it as an independent product. Here's how to start.

➤ Microsoft: www.microsoft.com.

Go to Microsoft's Web site and type the words "Photo Story" in the on-site search box. The resulting URL is a long string, so it's best that you go this route to find it. Bookmark the page for future review, or download Photo Story 3 immediately.

Next, follow this eight-step tutorial to create your own video.

1. Determine the video's message. Instructional, informative, educational, or overviews of products and/or services are good starter options.
2. Gather photos for your video, or begin taking photographs for the marketing message.
3. Download Photo Story 3 and become familiar with the software.
4. Create a script that matches each photo as the video progresses. The script need not be extensive. One or two sentences per photograph that describe the visual is all that's needed.
5. Add the first three to five photographs into Photo Story 3 to test the product and your voice narration as each photo changes. This is the phase where microphone adjustments and photo manipulation take place.
6. Select Windows Media Player, Real Player, or another popular media product to integrate within your video. Photo Story 3 provides a tutorial with instructions. Choose the player that's most familiar to clients.
7. Add beginning or ending royalty-free music to your video if it is beneficial to the message and welcomed by viewers. Do not add music if sounds other than your voice are distracting.

8. Review the finished work. Are you satisfied with the results, or are changes required? Edits are easily done without creating a new video. You can change the photo order and edit the voice narration for individual photographs instead of the entire video. Customize the product in a manner that's best suited to market what you sell. Then distribute the work in one of the six suggested formats. Make as many videos as you wish on numerous subjects, all free of charge and customizable to market to individuals and business clients.

Web Camera or Camcorder

Many entrepreneurs add video recording equipment to their marketing arsenal because allowing prospects to see a visual message or providing clients with help through a video tutorial is a powerful sales tool. Video creation elevates your firm above all competitors who do not utilize video in their marketing. The quickest method to start the process is through a webcam or camcorder.

A Web camera, or webcam, is usually mounted above your computer's monitor. Its position allows you to be in front of the camera to record your motions while speaking to the audience. If there's no need for you to walk from one room to another while speaking, a webcam may work to your advantage. However, if your message is best created similar to a movie, conducting interviews, or through multiple scenes, a camcorder is the more appropriate option.

There's a cost for each product, from an average of $49 for a webcam to $500 or more for a camcorder, depending on the model and manufacturer. Accessories may also be required, such as computer cables or a camcorder tripod. The investment is worth the money as long as you've set goals to grow your business through this medium.

Limit each video's length to no more than three to five minutes, except in cases where you're teaching a course or conducting a seminar. Individuals who watch videos prefer information delivered quickly. Their patience wanes quickly, so get to the point promptly. Consider creating a series of videos as an introduction to or a promotion of your for-sale products.

Each webcam and camcorder is sold with an instruction manual. Follow it to install the product and verify its compatibility with your computer. The most taxing yet fulfilling part comes next: creating test videos with your equipment as you prepare the finished product for Internet promotion. This step will take some time to master, and no doubt you'll feel the urge to do everything right the first time. But that's highly unlikely. As you work on this project, remember the phrase, "You only get one chance to make a first impression." It will take several attempts to videotape a session that you're proud to show on the Web.

My first computer experience was completed after sixteen tapings. At that point I grew tired of trying to live up to my inflated expectations and simply put together a three-minute video that I knew would please the audience.

There are two ways to upload (transfer from your computer to the Internet) your video, depending on where it will reside.

1. Follow the transfer directions provided by your webcam or camcorder's instruction book. If you are adding the video straight to your Web site, you may also need to read the instructions provided by your Web host.
2. Upload video directly to one of the popular video-sharing sites, such as MySpace.com or YouTube.com. These sites require you to open a free account before adding your video to the space that's provided to you through your account. Once your videos are added, the video-sharing site (which is now your video's host) will provide you with coding to place a still picture of the video clip on your business Web site or in any environment that allows visitors to click and watch the video.

The number of video-sharing sites increases every day. Use a search engine to broaden your choices. Also look at the other Web sites to learn which service they use. You'll usually find the video host's name at the top or bottom of the screen that surrounds the video.

Creating videos costs you time and/or money, but the additional promotion and revenue generated through this visual medium makes the investment worthwhile.

Podcasts

In 2001 Excite.com allowed Web visitors to create their own free, online radio show. A microphone was required. The Web site let you post the date and time of your broadcast on the Excite.com radio show's home page for the world to see twenty-four hours a day. This was revolutionary. I wrote a press release about my groundbreaking show, which still exists in Web archives. I also promoted information about the broadcast on my Web site.

FYI: Sample radio show press release.
www.prweb.com/releases/2001/6/prweb25917.htm.
Podcasting. http://en.wikipedia.org/wiki/Podcasting.

Excite.com canceled the broadcasting area just weeks after I started using it, but the introduction experience gave me an introduction to a marketing tool that attracted Web-based listeners. Today this broadcasting tool is known as the podcast, named in part for the wildly famous iPod and for the word "broadcast" in shortened form.

Podcasts have been created to discuss many topics, but the technology is still considered new. There's lots of room for growth, which is good for home-based and solo business owners ready to market their products and services through the spoken word.

Is Podcasting for You?

Podcast creation is open to every solo business owner, but everyone will not participate. Some business owners work in industries where prospects and clients have no time or interest in listening to an online broadcast. They prefer reading text or visiting a Web site. But some options might actually turn clients into podcast fans, allowing you to educate and inform through this verbal marketing process. Here are two possibilities.

- Let's say you offer a manual that clients order by mail or e-mail, but they need additional instruction. A podcast can act as a tutorial assistant, with accompanying screen shots posted on your Web site. Using Photo Story 3 is also acceptable, but a podcast may provide more clarity.
- You need to make special reports and speeches available in numerous formats, including CD and text. A podcast is another option for clients who are familiar with this technology.

How Difficult Is Podcasting?

New technology that forces you to download several products and integrate them before they supposedly work together is not what I consider simple and easy. Podcast options are posted all over the Web, such as articles and tutorials provided by podcasters and others who make audio tools available. Many convince you that there are too many steps to this process. For example, Yahoo!'s podcasting section provides a three-step tutorial, but you still must put together the pieces to create a podcast using various products not available directly through Yahoo!. That's why podcasting has been a mystery for most of us, until now.

FYI: Yahoo! podcasts. http://podcasts.yahoo.com/publish. **How to podcast.** www.how-to-podcast-tutorial.com

Podango: www.podango.com. TalkShoe: www.talkshoe.com

If you market to an audience that's on the go, that prefers listening to information through a computer, or that downloads music or online talk shows to portable devices, then it's time to consider communicating with these potential customers through podcasting.

A podcast is a talk show that you develop and distribute online. There are three steps to become a podcaster. You 1) record the content using a microphone and podcast recording site (such as Podango and TalkShoe in the FYI above), 2) convert the recording into an MP3 file, and 3) upload the podcast to your Web site or blog for easy access by listeners.

Podcasts are often created for music enthusiasts, but this quick tutorial focuses on how to attract an audience who looks forward to hearing your broadcasts. Here's how to proceed.

1. *Give your show a catchy name.* The title should describe the content so that listeners understand the focus before they tune in.

2. *Determine the show's length, format, and frequency.* Professional broadcasters stay within preset boundaries, and following that professional model will work for you. Choose a length from fifteen to twenty minutes, a format that uses one host (you) or a host and guest, and a weekly or monthly production timetable. These are reasonable strategies for the first-time podcaster.

3. *Research the competition.* Do other podcasts on your topic exist? If so, make a list of them and the formats they follow, using the points under step 2 as a guide. Resist canceling your podcast just because someone else hosts a similar program. There's room for one more participant within your industry.

4. *Record multiple podcasts consecutively.* Just because your show is broadcast once a week or month doesn't mean that's when you must record it. For efficiency's sake, plan and produce several shows at the same time.

5. *Invite industry suppliers to sponsor your podcast.* Firms are constantly searching for new methods to reach customers. Help them to understand how partnering with you to distribute podcasts will increase their exposure to a new audience.

Use search engines to find podcasting recording options and accessories, including intro and ending music, that give your broadcast a true radio-station experience.

Most of all, ask yourself one question before you begin podcasting: "How will I maximize the distribution of my podcasts with minimum effort?" The answer sets in motion your plan to grow an audience that views you as the leading authority in your field.

Frequently Asked Questions

We've reviewed four high-tech methods to inform your audience about your expertise and thus indicate what they can expect when buying your products or hiring you for the job. Here's the fifth method: Compile a list of frequently asked questions, or FAQs, for distribution in text format, on CD, or on the Web.

Newspapers, magazines, and other media sources feature FAQs as part of their weekly formats. Readers appreciate quick-to-read tutorials for products they own or for learning about services that save them time and money, streamline their workload, and allow them to prosper by knowing the ins and outs of specific industries.

People with whom you want to work become more confident about your skills when they see your knowledge highlighted through a series of simple questions and answers. FAQs also encourage prospects and clients to buy more of what you sell or upgrade what they currently use.

The marketing options using FAQs are expansive. Here are a few examples.

Text FAQs

Create a trifold brochure listing a series of your industry's most asked questions. FAQs created by firms in other industries give you an idea of how to structure your answers so that you don't give away the most coveted information. Clients will appreciate your insights but will not be able to handle the hardest jobs. They'll call you for that part of the service.

Web FAQs

Start a section on your Web site listing the top-ten questions clients ask. These FAQs can be the same as the ones featured in the trifold brochure. Write and edit the responses, then post them on your site.

CD FAQs

Some clients prefer to receive information in electronic format. That's where putting your FAQ details on CD works best. This product is useful when offering prospects free literature to review before calling for an appointment or writing an order. It's also beneficial to send as a follow-up to a meeting.

Consumer and Trade FAQs

Trade magazines and consumer newspapers often need information—basic or complex—to inform and inspire their audience. Customize your FAQs for both types of readers. Once they publish your FAQs, these media sources have the potential to create a new source of revenue that you would not have found otherwise.

Podcast FAQs

Creating an online radio show may not be in your short-term goals, but if it is, FAQs should be part of your podcast segments. A question-and-answer topic can be a regular format at the end of the show. Another FAQ segment can be structured as expert advice, such as the topic "Ten Ways to Distinguish a Real Diamond from a Fake." After you share the tip, tell listeners where they can find more FAQs on your Web site or blog.

FAQs are the educational component of your business. Neglecting to create and distribute them as part of your marketing campaign is similar to leaving money on the table. In today's fast-paced marketplace, that's not an affordable option.

Getting the word out to customers is one aspect of marketing. The products you use to distribute that information is another. The marketing ideas introduced in this chapter help to uncover prospects that you did not know exist in places not considered part of the search. These low-cost items get prospects' attention and keep current clients depending on your support.

Most marketers will try one or two of the easiest solutions first, not all of the ideas at once. Apply that strategy yourself, keeping track of results and moving forward to gain new customers who trust your opinion and depend on your expertise.

The following worksheet helps you decide which of these technological tools are right for your firm.

Marketing Products under Consideration Worksheet

(Place checkmarks where appropriate)

Marketing Product	Integrate into Plan Now	Consider at a Later Date	Not a Good Fit	Other Comments
Teleseminars				
Directories				
Web Videos				
Podcasts				
FAQs				

07 Internet Help to the Rescue

The media talk as if every business on the planet had a Web site. But that isn't true. If you are part of the group that doesn't yet have an Internet presence, is it too late to create a Web identity? Not at all. But it is time to begin your journey to establish a serious Web presence.

You may have tried to create an Internet site in the past, or perhaps someone was supposed to help you get online, but things didn't work out. Opportunities for getting online have changed drastically for the better, so you'll be able to get a site up and running on your own. At the very least you'll know your options and be able to move forward with this important element of running and marketing a business.

Getting on the Web is affordable these days. I created my first Web site in 1997 when the technology was in its infancy. Maintaining my site used to cost me $1,170 per year; now it costs $120, and that includes a shopping cart and blogging capabilities, two subjects explored later in this chapter. Some Web hosts (the companies that keep your site's presence on the Internet) provide service for less than the $120 I pay. This chapter will help you find such companies.

At the end of this chapter, you'll be ready to create an online presence, notify search engines of your address, and focus on bringing visitors to your virtual door.

FYI: Web host definition. http://en.wikipedia.org/wiki/Web_host. **Blog definitions.** http://en.wikipedia.org/wiki/Blog. www.marketingterms.com/dictionary/blog.

In a nutshell, the five steps you'll take to get online and market your site's existence are:

1. Choose a Web site name, and register it with an Internet registration company.
2. Research Web site hosts, weighing each company's benefits. Then decide on a host provider.
3. Select a Web creation software package. The easiest choices are:
- Using a host that makes customizable, online templates available.
- Making a blog template your primary Web site.
- Bypassing the Web host's templates in favor of Web page software.
4. Review industry-based Web sites to determine the strengths and weaknesses. Look at Web sites outside of your industry for ideas to make your site a place that visitors return to often.
5. Determine the best methods to create awareness, increase site traffic, track visitors, and capture sales.

Now let's look at these five steps in detail.

Step 1: Select and Register Your Web Site's Name

FYI: Uniform resource locator (URL) Definition. www.webopedia.com/TERM/U/URL.html.

A Web site name is the address that online users type into an Internet browser to find information about a particular industry, hobby, news event, and thousands of other topics. The site's address is known in technological terms as a uniform resource locator, or URL. Your first choice for a business-related URL is the actual name of your business. One of my companies, Sweet Survival, uses the Web address www.SweetSurvival.com. The name was available at the time of registration. Another choice is to register your own name. I registered the URL www.ShirleyFrazier.com. When individuals are searching for information on me, that's the first address they will consider typing into their Internet browser. Millions of Web names have been claimed, and many are being registered as you read this book. But don't let that deter you from researching and claiming your preferred URL.

Another smart option that solo and home-based business owners choose is to register name differentiations and extensions. A company such as Coca-Cola may choose to protect its brand by registering the Coca-Cola URL with .com, .net, and .org, the top three extensions of choice for name registration. These choices are also open to you as you select registration names for your site.

In time you may find that registering multiple extensions and name variations isn't worth the cost, but it's wise to consider doing so at the beginning. Later on you can determine whether to continue paying for the additional names or to drop them.

If the name you desire is taken, registration

Shirley Says

Who Registers URL Names?

There are many domain name registrants on the Internet. The most popular and best-known companies are Network Solutions (www.networksolutions.com), Register.com, and GoDaddy.com. Visit online to check the availability of and registration for your preferred URL. You will see price differences between the companies, but don't assume that a lower-priced company is less useful than higher-priced ones. All of them register URLs in the same manner and on the same level.

Network Solutions and Register.com charge $34.99 and $35.00 per year, respectively, to register your Web site name, while GoDaddy.com charges $8.95 per year. All three offer the same registration service. When visiting each site, you will also find a host of services that can be bundled with name registration, such as Web hosting, access to e-mail boxes, and search engine submission assistance. You can pay for services through these firms, or you can look for another host that provides lots of Web site space, e-mail capabilities, blogging tools, and more for similar or lower costs than the three companies named here.

firms will suggest other options, including hyphens between words (www.your-web-name.com), the letter "e" (electronic) in front of the name (www.eyourwebname.com), and the word "online" in back of the name (www.yourwebnameonline.com).

Another possible Web name is one based on the product or service you sell. My site Sweet Survival is the place where individuals learn about starting a gift basket business. Visitors can find the site by typing the URL www.SweetSurvival.com, or they can use the alternate address, www.Gift BasketBusiness.com. The latter is easier for most people to remember, as it focuses on the site's purpose. The memorability of a name is something to consider when searching for a Web name and alternate URLs.

A URL in any format other than the choices mentioned above is an outdated format not in your best interest. Your site's name should follow the pattern "www.yoursitename.com" rather than "www.yoursitename.hostname.com."

Step 2: Research Host Sites

Which companies will provide you with the most in service and amenities for the best price? As you research sites, complete the Web Host Comparison Worksheet to help identify Web hosts with the best deal for the features you desire. Here are the services and features that most solo and home-based business owners request.

- Web site storage space of 20 megabytes and up.

FYI: Megabyte definition. www.webopedia.com/TERM/m/megabyte.html.

- A minimum of ten e-mail boxes (many hosts are generous, providing twenty or more). Most businesses need multiple e-mail boxes so that each box can be used for a different function or service (help@yourwebname.com, orders@yourwebname,com, yourname@yourwebname.com, etc.).

Web Host Comparison Worksheet

FEATURES	NAME OF HOST			
	Host 1	Host 2	Host 3	Host 4
Setup fees (yes or no)				
Monthly or yearly cost				
Available number of subdomains (alternate Web names that can be linked to the main URL)				
Amount of available Web space (in megabytes)				
Number of e-mail accounts				
Spam filtering?				
Virus scanning?				
Blogging capabilities (yes or no)				
Shopping cart with SSL protection (yes or no)				
Statistics capabilities (yes or no)				
Internal firewall protection (site security on their servers) (yes or no)				
On-site tutorials (yes or no)				
24/7 support (yes or no) By telephone? By e-mail?				

- A secure shopping cart to sell an unlimited amount of products and services. Some Web hosts provide access to one shopping cart, while others give you five or more carts that are customizable with your logo, product or service photos, and the ability to collect payments through credit cards and alternative payment collectors, along with other amenities.
- The option to create 1) a site using the host's built-in templates, or 2) a site set up as a blog, which is also part of the host's system.
- Visitor tracking support through internal Web statistics. Some hosts provide detailed statistics on the numbers of Web site visitors, how they found you, and which pages they visited, while other hosts' statistics are woefully inadequate, providing scant information on visitors and popular pages. If everything else is adequate through your preferred host, statistics can be gathered through free, online sources that use charts and forms to provide a complete, statistical picture.
- Service on request. No Web host is worth the price if you are unable to get support by telephone or e-mail when you have questions or concerns about your Web hosting plan or specific features. A good Web host will make a fre-

quently asked questions (FAQ) area available on its site to answer general queries. However, you'll want to contact a live person by phone or expect a prompt response by e-mail if a problem occurs that isn't addressed in the FAQs.

Unfortunately, you won't know if you've chosen a Web host with good service until you need to contact customer support, and by then you've already signed on as a client. One way to find a good Web host is to ask colleagues about their host experiences. Another is to consult message boards and blogs on the Internet for opinions, taking what you read with a grain of salt, knowing that one individual who is dissatisfied is not representative of everyone hosted through that firm.

Step 3: Select Web Site Creation Software

There were few industry competitors in my field when I created my first site in 1997. I chose Microsoft FrontPage software to design the site because I read about its ease of use and the fact that it didn't require Web coding knowledge, also known as HTML. Still, I anticipated a steep learning curve and didn't look forward to understanding a new language just to create a Web site.

FYI: Hypertext markup language (HTML).
www.w3.org/MarkUp/. **Secure socket layer (SSL).**
www.webopedia.com/TERM/S/SSL.html.

The hosting company I chose offered a shopping cart, which I customized for receiving orders online. But the cart wasn't secure from access to credit card numbers by unscrupulous people. I had to apply to an outside firm to add an SSL certificate that encrypted each client's credit card number when entered into my cart. When orders arrived, I processed the credit card information through a terminal in my office. This in-office terminal had been set up with help from my bank years before I established an online presence. I used my printer to print the order from the computer and manually processed the transaction.

That procedure is still maintained in my office, but you now have other choices. Today there are online merchants that handle transactions for you. This streamlines the order processing and places the funds, minus transaction fees, into the bank account of your choice.

I was pleasantly surprised with my Web page software experience and am just as pleased that today's Web site hosts make templates available. This allows you get up and running on the Web much more quickly than it took years ago.

Web hosts not only broadcast your Web site on the Internet, they also provide the tools to create a site that's informative, interesting, and attractive. No more "under construction" signs or blank home pages announcing your forthcoming site. Choose a Web host, receive your user name and password by e-mail within minutes after sign-up, and follow the host's instructions to begin creating a site.

FYI: Popular blog programs. Blogger: www
.blogger.com. TypePad: www.typepad.com.
WordPress: www.wordpress.org.

In most cases you'll be given the choice to create your pages as a traditional Web site or as a blog. Either choice is acceptable, depending on the structure you want and tools that are required to showcase what you have to offer visitors. There's one main difference. A blog turns each text entry on your Web pages into a communication device, allowing visitors to insert comments. A traditional Web site does not provide that capability.

Both traditional Web sites and blogs can be set up with narrow columns on the left and right side of each page. These columns are called sidebars. Here is where you add a site table of contents and off-site page links to valuable information that complements your site's contents.

You can also create your site by using Web page software purchased at retail stores or through online sellers or downloaded from the manufacturer's computer to yours. This software has been available for as long as the Internet has existed. Although online templates are popular Web site choices, software will continue to play a role in site creation and be chosen by individuals who either have familiarity with the product or feel more comfortable working with it.

Microsoft FrontPage and Macromedia Dreamweaver are said to be easy-to-use software packages. Because the templates provided by Web hosts are so simple to arrange, it is wise to work with them first if you're not familiar with Web page software.

FYI: **Web page software.** Microsoft FrontPage: www.microsoft.com/frontpage. Macromedia Dreamweaver: www.macromedia.com/software/dreamweaver.

All software is accompanied by a manual explaining how to install and use the product. However, not all manuals are written in a user-friendly format, and that leads many users to consult easy-to-understand tutorials available online and in books from libraries and bookstores. Do not hesitate to review these additional sources for help.

Setting Up Your Shopping Cart

The ability to link a shopping cart to a site, offering customers a way to pay online for goods and services, was once a cost over and above the initial Web site investment. But things have changed for the better. Web hosts now bundle shopping carts with basic Web services. These carts are licensed to Web hosts, allowing users to take advantage of a cart's encrypted technology to add whatever you sell while capturing the buyer's personal information and credit card number.

Some carts are still not totally customizable. There are times when you must manually adjust shipping costs applied to an order when it arrives in your in-box, but most other functions are controllable.

You aren't necessarily locked into using your Web host's cart, especially if another type of cart seems to be a better solution for the items you sell. Perhaps you sell many reports that are downloaded and delivered directly by e-mail after a customer pays. Instead of manually processing the order in your office and physically sending the report through your computer, you can find an online service whose shopping carts handle the online report delivery and place the revenue into the bank account of your choice, minus fees. If this streamlined method is for you, carts exist that make selling a hands-free process.

Most of all, online shopping carts are evolving as quickly as the Internet, and that's good news for solo and home-based owners with lots of projects and limited time.

Step 4: Review Other Web Sites

There's no doubt that other people in your industry have set up sites on the Web. Your mission is to locate your industry partners and competitors, bookmarking their sites so that you can review them meticulously to uncover their strengths and weaknesses. This will help you to decide what's best to include on your site and how to move forward adding that information.

FYI: Bookmark definition. http://en.wikipedia .org/wiki/Bookmark.

No two Web sites are alike, even when they're part of the same industry or address the same topic. That's why looking at sites that are *outside* of your industry give you a well-rounded focus on what may work to make your site a unique place that piques visitors' initial interest and brings them back periodically to see what's new.

Consider the Web sites that you've bookmarked as part of your favorites. What makes those sites special enough for bookmarking, and how can you add that ingenuity to your forthcoming site?

Hopefully, you already have a vision regarding your site structure and layout. Here's a list of pages to consider creating as you get ready to put your business on the Internet.

Home page. Includes an introduction to the site, reason why the site is a primary source for goods and services on a particular topic, and summary of what visitors will find on subsequent pages.

"What's new" page. Informs about recent updates on the site that visitors may not know exist.

Frequently asked questions page. Contains basic questions and answers about your business, its policies and terms of service, and general information about the industry in which you participate.

Products and services page. Provides information on items and/or consulting help made available to site visitors.

Articles or tips pages. A document or documents, written in a long or short format by you or another knowledgeable party, that educates visitors on industry details that make your product or service valuable.

Newsletter subscription page. Allows and encourages visitors to subscribe to your online weekly or monthly publication.

Different types of information are critical to every business Web site, and these six pages begin to mold your site into a place where expert material and advice is found by individuals looking for ideas and solutions.

Use photographs and graphic images as sparingly or frequently as required to make your site interesting and attractive.

As you decide on your Web site's structure, try not to become overwhelmed by the options. You don't want an unorganized site with pages that confuse and repel visitors. Choose a few strong options at the outset and keep other opportunities in your pocket. In the coming years you'll change the site's template and structure to reflect the content that visitors want most. On-site and informal surveys will help you uncover how to make your site a magnet, attracting worldwide visitors who look to you for news, ideas, and products that benefit their personal or business life.

Step 5: Create Site Buzz on a Budget

Making individuals aware of your Web site is a matter of persistence. You may complete many objectives within a week to let people know you exist. However, it will take many more days—or months—to get the publicity train up to speed. The easiest methods you can put into place immediately are: 1) creating awareness by submitting your site to search engines, 2) increasing site traffic by leaving your signature on sites where people want to know more about your expertise, 3) tracking Web site visitors (where they come from and where they migrate on your site), and 4) capturing sales by convincing visitors about the benefits of associated products.

Creating Awareness

A good part of your research has been spent on the Web looking at competitive sites, as mentioned earlier. Once you've uploaded your site onto the Web, you'll want to contact the major search engines about your presence.

There are hundreds of search engines on the Web, but only a few need be contacted. Look for the "submit your site" link on the home page of these search engines, and follow the directions for submission.

FYI: Search engine definition. www.webopedia .com/TERM/s/search_engine.html. **Ping (packet Internet grouper) definition.** http://en.wikipedia.org/ wiki/Ping.

If you create your site using a blog template, submission is not necessary. Each time you post to the blog portion of your site, a ping (a notification between computers that your blog was recently updated) is generated, alerting search engines that new content is available. Blogs normally contain a ping option automatically built in to the template. This eliminates the site submission process. Just make sure that your blog setup has the ping process installed and each new post includes a checked field that verifies search engines are contacted when new content is uploaded.

Increasing Site Traffic

Another part of your research will uncover places where people are apt to be interested in your site's focus. Such places include e-mail signatures, blogs, and message boards.

E-mail Signatures

FYI: Signature (SIG) Definition. www.marketing terms.com/dictionary/sig_file/.

Most e-mail programs allow you to create a custom signature, also known as a SIG file, which appears each time you write or respond to an e-mail. This signature is a call to action about something relevant you wish to share with individuals, convincing them to visit your site or blog, subscribe to a newsletter, sign up for a complimentary appointment, receive a free report, and and select many other benefits to visitors.

A maximum of three links is appropriate within a custom e-mail signature. It's enough to give visitors a glimpse into what you offer and not so much that confusion stops them from clicking on the highlighted links.

Here's a sample signature found at the end of an e-mail message:

```
===================================
Solo Business Marketing
Where entrepreneurs and success connect
www.SoloBusinessMarketing.com
Voice: (973) 279-2799

Subscribe to the SoloSmarts weekly newsletter
www.solobusinessmarketing.com/newsletter.htm

Is working solo for you? Take our mini course.
www.solobusinessmarketing.com/course.htm
===================================
```

Look for the custom signature link within your e-mail program. Create your own signature, reviewing and refining it until you are pleased with its message.

Message Boards

A signature at the end of a message board post is similar to an e-mail SIG file. It may be shorter than the one shown above, but it's usually not longer. Like the e-mail signature, the message board end signature is meant to provide readers with additional information about what can be found on your site.

In both cases this self-serving message should be more informational than advertorial. Savvy Web site surfers know the difference between both and are more apt to click on the link if it leads to a source that shares information rather than tries to sell a product or service. Not all signature creators follow this rule, but it's best to develop trust with other posters, especially if you are a frequent message-board participant.

Blog Posts

A different type of signature, other than one shown in an e-mail or on a message board, is expected when you leave a blog post comment. The link created at the top of a blog post that highlights your name is the only type of signature that's acceptable. An example is: "*Shirley George Frazier* says." On the Internet, the name is underlined to reflect a clickable link to a site affiliated with the writer who adds a comment.

While this information is general to most blogs, reviewing comments at blogs where you wish to participate will tell you whether typing information similar to a SIG file or the traditional name link is appropriate.

In creating awareness for and increasing traffic on your Web site, the best etiquette is to follow the example of others who have created their own form of Web branding when sharing ideas in participatory environments. When your own site, message board, or blog is up and running, you can set rules or remind participants of the rules related to message sharing in the space you've created.

Tracking Visitors

One of the most important ways to bring visitors to your site and keep them coming back is to know how they found their way to your site in the first place. Did they arrive through a link at another site? Did a news report featuring your Web site create the connection? Did someone click on a link you added to a message board or blog post? You won't always know the exact answer, but there will be signs that point you in the right direction to learn how your site was found.

Site analytics programs reveal how people find you on the Web. These statistical programs for your Web site tell you which pages visitors reviewed and the length of each visit. The programs help you capitalize on site traffic and understand the hot-button issues, articles, products, and overall content that interest visitors.

Analytics programs reveal many types of data about your site, including:

- How visitors access the site (direct, Web links, search engine, etc.)
- The number of new visitors and returning visitors
- Pages on your site that are popular and pages that are not
- The number of visitors per day, week, month, and year
- The geographic location of site visitors (by U.S. state or worldwide country)

Some statistics programs are basic, disclosing minimum information about site visitors, while others display extensive details in the form of charts and graphs. Program costs do not determine how deep the data is mined. There are many free programs that provide a wealth of statistical material. Type the words "analytics program" into a search engine to find tracking software that works for you.

These programs require that you add a line of coding to your Web site pages so that they can capture statistical information. This process is easy; most programs provide diagrams or instructions to help you add coding in the correct format. Today's free statistics programs don't require a link back to their site, nor do you need to add a large logo to your site in exchange for using the technology. Some programs require a small icon/logo, one that does not intrude on your Web site's real estate. Other programs are undetectable on your site.

Turning Visitors into Customers

Convincing prospects to take one step forward, from browsing your site to purchasing through the online shopping cart, takes just a few minutes for some visitors and weeks for others. Your site must be a combination of helpful information and influential text, providing enough of a comfort zone to put visitors at ease, elevating their trust level to buy your products and services.

What features convince visitors to trust you and place orders?

1. A money-back guarantee.
2. A prominently displayed business address, telephone number, and e-mail address for questions before or after the purchase.
3. A trial consultation (usually twenty to thirty minutes).
4. Testimonials from satisfied customers.

5. Evidence of your prominence and expertise, developed through years of industry participation.

Every business cannot offer all five "comfort factors," but two or three are often enough to get the sale. Review the online shopping benefits offered by your competition as posted in their printed literature and on their Web sites. Do competitors post none of these benefits? Then you should be first to offer them, which could sway their prospects to buy from you. Don't be surprised if the competition follows your lead, posting a list of benefits that mirrors or competes with your own.

Electronic Newsletters Keep Clients Connected

You've set up your Web site and installed a shopping cart. This is just the beginning of your journey to create an environment that clients and prospects visit as often as possible. After the initial launch, contact prospective visitors using postcards and other mailed literature as discussed in chapter 3. Another way to get their attention is to publish an electronic newsletter.

FYI: E-newsletter definitions. Wikipedia: http://en.wikipedia.org/wiki/Enewsletter.

Electronic newsletters inform anyone interested in your Web site about what's of interest and why they should visit. This e-newsletter, as it's named on the Internet, contains news and ideas that appeal to readers. It is created using one of many templates provided by host firms specializing in e-newsletter creation and delivery to subscribers' e-mail addresses. The host firm also makes HTML code available so that interested parties can subscribe to and unsubscribe from your publication and so that you can get detailed publishing statistics on such things as the number of subscribers, how many e-newsletters were opened versus not opened, and which e-mail addresses bounced.

Your e-newsletter format will depend on what subscribers want to read, and the same is true for its length. Some readers have time to absorb long newsletters, while others need short, concise publications that lead them back to more information found on your site. In many cases, the latter version is more valuable, since the purpose of a newsletter is to increase your Web site's readership and overall popularity.

What type of information makes readers anticipate your e-newsletter?

- Original articles on your specific topic.
- Tips that readers can use immediately.
- Ideas generated by clients who ask questions by phone or e-mail.

What details help you to market your business and sell to readers?
- Information on new products or services and where to find details on your site.
- Notification of items on sale in your online store.

- Links to hot topics being discussed on your blog.

An e-newsletter costs less to deliver than its direct mail counterpart, as mentioned in chapter 3, but not all clients or industries use online newsletters as the main method of contact.

As mentioned, getting subscribers to return to your Web site is the main reason for publishing an e-newsletter. But there are more uses. An e-newsletter:

- Announces new Web site areas that subscribers may have overlooked. Site visitors sometimes fail to see new features, even if the news is posted on the home page or a "what's new" page. An e-newsletter is another avenue to tell readers what they may not recognize.
- Lets you interact with subscribers, asking them for opinions and other feedback. Announcing a survey (see chapter 3) is one way to compile their comments, providing you with immediate responses on a pending idea.
- Gives you a method to increase online sales. Most e-newsletter publishers include one or several offers. The publication is being sent to people who have subscribed willingly. Why not market your goods to the best buying candidates?
- Creates a blog following. Subscribers may not visit your blog as often as you wish. An e-newsletter keeps them up to date on blog topics to read and share ideas.
- Encourages readers to subscribe to a complementary print newsletter. If you publish a newsletter sent by direct mail that provides

information not featured on your Web site or expands on the e-newsletter's topics, the online newsletter is the perfect place to drum up print version sales.

Content Development and Other Concerns

- How well do you know your clients? The more you understand their preferences, the more successful you'll be at reaching them through your publication. Even if you've taken time to query clients, it can still take months to refine your e-newsletter, its format, and frequency. But the sooner you begin to lay a foundation, the quicker it will become part of your marketing campaign.

- Will the e-newsletter be published in long or short format? Many publishers start with longer formats that mirror newspapers and magazines. If your e-newsletter's internal statistics show that readers open it consistently, you'll know that the longer version is working. If open rates are low, try a shorter version. Reduce the text by including only the first few sentences or paragraphs of an article; use a link to take readers to the rest of the story on your site. The last line of your articles might offer a product or service in conjunction with the subject.

- Are graphics an attention grabber, or is plain text best? The answer depends on many factors. Some e-newsletter readers are thrilled by visuals. It inspires them to quickly open the link. In some cases, your e-newsletter host may not allow you to add graphics. Another consideration is the rate at which e-mail hosts bar graphic-based publications from being delivered to in-boxes. E-mail hosts sometimes screen text-only e-newsletters, but because mail with graphics tends to bloat the e-mail's size, it is often treated as spam unless the subscriber adds your e-newsletter's name to their approved sender's list. You can encourage this action on your subscription page.

If graphics are important, but you do not or cannot add them to your e-mailed newsletter, a link within the publication can lead readers to a graphic version on your Web site, which you create without help from the e-newsletter host. You may wonder why the on-site newsletter is not considered as the main publication rather than using an e-newsletter host. The answer is simple. You're trying to bring visitors to your site. The best way to do this is through e-mail contact. The e-mail version leads visitors to your Web site, which increases readership and sales.

- Articles, tips, and ideas are what fill an e-newsletter, but where will you find this content if you're not an expert writer? Help lies in free article sites on the Web. Writers make articles on thousands of topics available online for use in your e-newsletter, on your Web site, and on your blog. The article must be used as written, which includes the writer's information box at the end. This is one source of content; there are others, such as questions that clients ask accompanied by your responses. Tips that you share in booklet format are still another. Clients perceive anything you write as more credible than a copy-and-paste article. Including your own content rather than using articles belonging to nonindustry participants elevates your status as a business, within the industry, or as a consumer ally. And be sure to review competitor's e-newsletters for ideas on where to find relevant content.

- How frequently will you publish the newsletter? Frequency is also an issue. Contacting clients weekly makes a positive impact for some in terms of readership and sales, but is a weekly format for you? It may be best to start the newsletter as a monthly, especially at the beginning if you're unsure of each issue's content and how readers will respond. Consider the frequency of competitive publications. The decision of how often to publish your e-newsletter is your choice.

Delivery and Costs

Once you decide on the publication's contents and frequency, it's time to find a host with templates and delivery tools. Search engines will help to uncover many e-newsletter hosts. Another technique is to look at the bottom of e-newsletters you admire. The host's logo is always found at the bottom. The logo is usually clickable, leading you straight to the host's home page for more investigation.

Most e-newsletter hosts let you try their services free of charge for at least one month. This lets you test the creation and delivery controls before committing to a long-term relationship.

This is a good feature. Fees for producing an e-newsletter are vastly different, depending on the host. One company may charge $100 for a year's service, while another charges $25 or more per month. There are many considerations when making your selection, including:

- Is there a wide range of templates from which to choose?
- Is the creation process easy?
- Can I include graphics?
- How many e-newsletters can I send for the monthly or yearly fee?
- Does the host provide me with the code that creates an online subscription box?
- How easy is it for me to import e-mail addresses I've collected into the host's system?
- How responsive is the host to my questions? (To test this, send at least two questions via e-mail during the trial process.)
- How extensive are each host's statistics, and which numbers do I really need?

You will pay the host to provide you with templates and means for delivery, but in most cases you will not charge your subscribers to receive the news. It's the price home-based and solo business owners pay to market. Treat the fees associated with publishing an online newsletter as an investment in your business rather than an expense. E-newsletters allow you to tell clients about products and services as well as act as a partner in their business or personal lives. Most of all, your e-newsletter must lead readers back to your Web site and/or blog as much as possible. That will ensure its overall success.

Don't be dismayed if your e-newsletter isn't distributed to thousands of subscribers. It's better to deliver to a few hundred buyers and referrals than thousands of browsers. Once my e-newsletter reaches the 1,000 subscribers range, I start looking at the mailing list to see who's opening it and who's not, unsubscribing anyone who has not opened my publication in three months. Delivery to each person costs money. I have the right to determine who receives my news. So do you.

Marketing Strategies

Making clients and prospects aware of your e-news can be accomplished on and off the Web. Here are five methods.

1. Use the HTML code provided by the host company to create an online subscription box. This template is to be pasted on most, if not all, of your Web site and blog pages. Many sites contain a header template that duplicates anything within the header region on every page. That will let you paste the subscription box once for duplication on each site or blog page. Try this procedure during the free trial subscription.
2. Create a dedicated subscription page on your Web site. This page will tell visitors why they should subscribe as well as provide the subscription box.

FYI: Sample subscription page.

www.solobusinessmaketing.com/newsletter.htm.

3. Notify clients by postcard. Starting an online newsletter gives you another reason to contact customers by direct mail. Postcards should also be sent to anyone who's shown interest in the past.
4. Include notice about the e-newsletter in your e-mail signature. Each time you send an e-mail, it will include a link to your subscription page. The procedure is explained later in this chapter.
5. Inform everyone about the newsletter on your business card, stationery, brochures, and other print literature.

Create a long-term vision for your e-newsletter before you begin. Publish your news for at least a year. Then decide to continue or end it. During that time, use surveys to learn how the publication can best serve its readers. This feedback also helps to elevate your motivation.

Creating an Online Press Room

An online press room, also known as a media room, should be part of your Web site. This virtual media kit works to market your business and industry expertise. The press room can be one or more pages, depending on the amount of information you share and how the data is separated. It also depends on your industry longevity. The longer you've been in business, the more expertise you'll post online. Here's an example of how to structure an online press room.

Index. This first page introduces the reader to the site and provides a breakdown of what's included on subsequent pages.

Backgrounder. The second page is a synopsis of your business and your experience—who you are, how and when the business began, milestones, and affiliated associations.

Press relations. The third page lets readers know which media—newspapers, magazines, television, radio, cable, and satellite—hosted your appearances and printed your expert quotes. Separate the details by media type. If links are available to online interviews, this is where you add links to those stories. A sample of this media room page is found at the end of the chapter.

Industry facts and figures. Share expertise about your industry by providing insights and statistics. Citings can be collected from your own surveys and from industry associations with access to statistics. Be sure to properly attribute outside sources.

Frequently asked questions. A list of ten to twelve questions and answers elevates your expertise. General questions, rather than technical, are best in this section. The information you provide here encourages the media to call for expert solutions and prospects to call for consultative projects. See a sample media room at www .solobusinessmarketing.com/mediaroom.htm.

Books, CDs, pamphlets. List the products that support your expertise. If you've written a book, whether self-published or through a traditional publisher, scan the cover and add it to the media room. Place the book's synopsis below the scanned cover. Customer comments about the book add relevance. Look for these comments in mailed correspondence, e-mailed notes, and online bookstores' comments sections if your book is sold through these sites.

The bottom of each media section page includes information on how to contact you. See how this is done in the sample media room page.

Photographs complement the text in your press room, so if you have photos that show interaction with customers or industry professionals, add those pictures on these pages. That will help to create an informative section visited by media, customers, and competitors.

Getting up-close and personal with media broadcasters taps into a powerful outlet that markets your message to a local, national, or international audience. Secure a publicist's help or pursue this marketing avenue on your own. Each broadcast segment has the potential to create a lifetime of sales.

We've covered a lot of ground in this chapter. Establishing your Web site takes many steps. Rest assured—you have the ability to complete each step. No marketing plan can move forward without an Internet presence. List your goals, complete the objectives, set up your e-newsletter, create an online press room, and begin reaping the rewards that occur when the Web becomes part of your everyday life.

CLIENT LIST, NEWS COVERAGE, SEMINAR LOCATIONS

OUR CLIENTS

Barnes & Noble

Macy's

MetLife

Main Cards & Gifts

TELEVISION APPEARANCES

CNBC

Food Network

Fox Channel 5 (NY)

New Jersey Network

NEWS COVERAGE

Newspapers

Birmingham Journal

Charlotte Observer

Chicago Tribune

Fort Worth Star-Telegram

New York Newsday

Orange County Register

Philadelphia Tribune Business

The Record (NJ)

SEMINAR LOCATIONS

Atlanta

Boston

Chicago

Dallas

Denver

Los Angeles

Miami

New York

Washington, DC

Magazines

Black Enterprise

Costco Connection

Entrepreneur Magazine Opportunity

Spare Time Magazine

Trade Magazines

Fancy Food

Florists' Review

Flowers&

Gifts & Decorative Accessories

Gourmet News

Contact Us

Comments

Share your opinion about this site on our comments page.

Partnerships

E-mail questions about business matters to Mike Hanna at mhanna@mysite.com.

Press

We are always happy to speak with the media. E-mail your questions to Henry Hudson, media manager at hhudson@mysite.com, or call (555) 893-1600 for fast response.

Our Location

Solo Business Marketing

P.O. Box 31, River Street Station

Paterson, NJ 07544-0031

Voice (973) 279-2799

Security Issues and Solutions

If you've just started a business, you may be surprised to realize how important security is in relation to marketing. But think about this: If you don't protect your property, whether online content or physical products, you will have little or nothing to market. This chapter looks at three types of small-business security issues: physical property, intellectual property, and computer data. We'll discuss copyrights, patents, trademarks, computer back-up systems, and other tools to protect you.

Perhaps you've never considered securing your products or intellectual property, or maybe you thought there was no available protection. Everything can be covered with some measure of security. It doesn't mean that someone won't duplicate your work, but it will slow them down or make a project too difficult to copy.

Security Problems from the Trenches

Marketing keeps you behind a desk, creating letters and brochures that offer and close deals. It also takes you out into the world to mingle with people who want to know more about your business and how it benefits them. Some home-based business owners love the interaction, while others shudder at the thought of leaving their offices to meet the public.

The truth of the matter is, business owners who want to be successful must occasionally leave the confines of their offices. Good businesspeople all seem to have one thing in common: They're keenly aware of the difference between people looking to buy and people looking to copy. Prospects look at the merchandise. You can almost see the wheels turning in their heads as they recognize how buying the item makes a tedious chore easier or a rough surface smoother. The copiers view an item with a completely different focus. Buying is not on this person's mind. This person wonders, "How can I copy this and make money from it?" You may have seen this expression, and perhaps the same has panned across your face in the past. We cannot stop anyone from duplicating our style and making minor changes, but we are able to create and implement security systems to protect materials that have taken years to perfect.

My sister, Cassandra, is an example of a security-conscious entrepreneur. She's in the cutthroat world of crafts. People who make items from scratch often develop ideas from what they see in magazines and craft show booths. Cassandra answers questions cautiously. Some booth visitors admit that they're also into crafts and proceed to ask proprietary questions. She won't respond, which forces the visitors to exit in search of another, less security-conscious crafter.

I was born with a trusting heart and flair for sharing the most minute details. It has been beneficial in the teaching arena but a weakness elsewhere. After books, CDs, and booklets were lifted several times from my own display tables, I finally learned how to secure my products, even when my back is turned.

Home-based and solo business owners market great ideas and products every day. Those same ideas and products need a built-in security system. Here are some examples.

Online

Photographs. Artists sell by displaying images of their work on Internet Web sites. They've learned that watermarks added on top of portraits and paintings decrease the chance of having the work lifted and posted elsewhere. A watermark can be removed, but it takes time and energy. Thieves pass over protected works in search of easier targets.

Articles and reports. Web site owners who educate visitors on everything from baby care to senior services make data available in article, report, and tip formats. Some material is general knowledge. Other data provide advice. Then there's intellectual material that is so coveted that it's best sold in text format on paper specially made to discourage duplication. This type of material includes statistics and industry data (upcoming trends on fashion, color, etc.).

Offline

Publications. Renting a booth at a trade or consumer show may be part of your marketing strategy. However, your blood may boil if you watch a person at your booth standing motionless, reading a sample of a for-sale report cover to cover, only to put it down and walk away. This is why some business owners do not exhibit at shows.

Technological data. It's difficult to protect all of your products while traveling alone. You bring products to sell at a particular event, and for the most part, everyone abides by the honor system of taking only what they plan to buy. But sometimes things get out of control, and you may be missing items that were not paid for, especially CDs and videotapes.

Physical Security

Home-based business owners who sell expensive products learn how to protect them while traveling to demonstrations and consumer shows. They use bars, locks, and cables that clamp onto surfaces. These supplies provide temporary security without damaging furniture. Even with this type of protection, these owners can share stories on how security was cut, stripped, or swiped along with the product.

Security isn't just a problem for expensive items. It's also required for anything you don't want to lose, no matter what the cost. As an example, your favorite pen is attached to a thin cord that stays around your neck. The pen emerges from its compartment when needed, but somehow it disappears. You look down at the cord to see a penless cap. Your own security has been breached. It's an unfortunate circumstance that may be small to some, but it's not to the person whose pen is missing.

Let's look at two more security issues from the trenches.

Trade Show Dilemmas

I've attended trade shows for more than fifteen years and have seen evidence of careless security in practically every aisle. The New York Incentive Rewards & Recognition Expo and the Motivation Show, two wonderful events that every marketer should attend (more on these shows in chapter 9), is where you can take free marketing samples from most booths. Personalized rubber bands, eye makeup remover, lotions, gift cards, chocolates, and logo-customized pens are some of the treasured items. I've seen attendees sweep their arms across a table in an attempt to deposit everything into their show bags. That's the type of security breech that occurs if an exhibitor isn't watching.

Solution:

Qualify each recipient to receive a sample product. This tactic works for exhibitors with a limited number of samples. I've seen this process for distributing gift cards, desk calendars, and plush items. Long lines form with attendees waiting their turn to speak with a representative and receive the coveted gift, if they qualify. But not all exhibitors go this route. Some have thousands of samples to distribute. Scattering items across a table to create a frenzy of excitement while fielding questions from inquisitive attendees works for them.

Another solution is to use empty containers or covers as visual stimulus. These let customers see what you're selling without having the real products on the table. Bring additional containers to replace any that disappear. This is an option for Roger Green of Teed Up in chapter 1 as he begins to create CDs and similar media. It's what I do when displaying products at a show.

Positioning Problems

As a home-based business owner, I travel by myself, but that doesn't mean I'm always alone. I have colleagues in California who accompany me to events where I speak about small business topics. The setting can be a small hotel meeting room or a cavernous convention hall. My friends provide top-notch security in places where I cannot control what happens at the buying table. One colleague followed a potential buyer as she drifted into a faraway corner with a book she hadn't yet purchased. Were the book's words so mesmerizing that she could not account for her actions? My friend retrieved the book which was, unfortunately, not purchased after the detailed inspection.

A different event resulted in a loss. Another colleague temporarily vacated a sales table to complete an order with a customer seated in front of the room. Books for sale and other items were positioned on the inside of a door. On the other side was a walkway used by hundreds of show attendees walking to other destinations. Two people walked in, grabbed books, and walked out. My friend was approaching the table when this occurred, and she chose not to raise her voice because of my ongoing presentation. She made the right decision but was upset because of the theft. Still, I could not have sold as much product on that day without her help.

Solution:

Prepare a sales form listing all items available at your event and distribute it to each attendee.

Add payment details (cash only, check payable details, etc.) and your Web site address as information for those who take the sheet but don't order. If a person considers making a purchase, the form will allow you to expedite the process without vacating the sales table. Providing customer service is one thing, but leaving the goods unmanned to focus on one customer is dangerous.

Creating a sales form takes little time, especially if you have a form on your Web site. Copy and paste it into a word processing document. Then make changes as needed and save the form for future events.

Let anyone who is ready to buy at a seminar do so at the table rather than from another location. It's impossible to secure multiple areas when you're one person, so don't try.

Intellectual Security: Paranoia Is Healthy

It's perfectly normal to be fearful about your work and other intellectual property being taken and used in a manner you did not approve. Such fear moves you to action. What type of registration is available? How can you guard against theft? Where are the tools, and are they affordable? These thoughts and many others run through your mind. There are methods that calm those fears, even if security is not available for everything.

United States Patent and Trademark Office: www.uspto.gov. United States Copyright Office: www.copyright.gov.

You may have heard that ideas cannot be protected. That is true. The U.S. Patent and Trademark Office (USPTO) states that "a trademark includes any word, name, symbol, or device, or any combination, used, or intended to be used, in commerce to identify and distinguish the goods of one manufacturer or seller from goods manufactured or sold by others, and to indicate the source of the goods." The same is true if you plan to apply for a copyright. The U.S. Copyright Office defines a copyright as, "a form of protection provided by the laws of the United States (title 17, U.S. Code) to the authors of 'original works of authorship,' including literary, dramatic, musical, artistic, and certain other intellectual works." This law applies to materials that are published or unpublished, but it does not apply to an idea.

Here's one of the key points, from the Copyright Office Web site, on what cannot be protected: "Ideas, procedures, methods, systems, processes, concepts, principles, discoveries, or devices, as distinguished from a description, explanation, or illustration." Still, there are many weapons within your reach to provide security in a broad sense.

Be aware that not everything needs security or is a candidate for the same type of protection. Janet Ross, the CPA in chapter 1, doesn't need to copyright the articles in her marketing brochures because she didn't write the content, and the entire product is made for her by an outsourcing firm. She does, however, need to protect her clients' accounting information. Hard copies of tax statements require storage in a waterproof

safe secured by a combination lock. Statements housed within her computer are accessed by a security code, and a backup set of clients' files were copied onto an external computer hard drive. Should her computer files become corrupted, the external drive provides a method for instant retrieval. Janet has also learned that some colleagues store clients' records on CD on a yearly basis, which is placed in a separate area from the waterproof safe files. Janet plans to do the same.

Roger Green, chapter 1's golf specialist, has no need to patent the golf clubs and supplies he sells. That's covered by the products' manufacturers. He does plan to trademark his business name, Teed Up. Roger will also create a guide to help other golf specialists start youth golf schools in other states. He believes the blueprint he's developed of working with school officials and parents will serve as a model that other areas can follow. A set of tutorial CDs to teach and train golf to youth and adults is also part of Roger's plan. When completed, the printed guide and CDs qualify as intellectual property securable through copyright.

These are examples of how home-based business owners take action to provide security to products and services they develop or maintain.

The following Product Creation Chart lists materials you may be developing or already have available and their corresponding types of protection. If you don't see items specific to your business, the respective Web sites for patents, trademarks, and copyrights will steer you in the right direction.

Product Creation Chart

Product or Service	Types of Protection			
	Copyright	Patent	Trademark	No Protection
Books, booklets, brochures, articles, and anything in written form	X			
CDs, videotapes, DVDs, anything in audio format	X			
Business name, product name			X	
Model or design element		X		
Music	X			
Architectural or similar drawings	X			
Choreographic work	X			
Inventions		X		
Symbols for identitfication			X	
Ideas, methods, systems, concepts				X

Quick Copyright Tips

Copyright protects most printed material. Once you've written a song, article, or training manual, it's your property and is copyrighted even if you choose not to pay for copyright protection. You may have heard of friends who practice their own type of security against claims, people who mail the materials to themselves and don't open it as a form of protection. At trade shows I've heard many attorneys who specialize in copyright law say that this practice isn't necessary. When a pen connects with any type of writing surface to form written content, the result is automatically your copyrighted material, unless the words are already someone else's property. (For example, the slogan "just do it" belongs to Nike, so don't try to claim it as part of your business name.) In fact, the Copyright Office's frequently asked questions section states that "your work is under copyright protection the moment it is created and fixed in a tangible form that it is perceptible either directly or with the aid of a machine or device." Obtain the services of an attorney versed in this topic if you require guidance.

If the time comes to sue another party for use of your material, a certificate of copyright issued by the U.S. Copyright Office provides you with a stronger case. You'll be able to prove what is yours and when it was copyrighted. That's the advantage over not registering your property, even though you can still go to court with uncopyrighted material to argue your case.

Visit the U.S. Copyright Office online and print out the correct form for the material you wish to protect. Forms can also be requested by mail or found and copied at local libraries. If you are copyrighting articles, tip sheets, or a booklet and are the only author, Short Form TX is what you require. If you want to register many articles or published works in one batch, use Form GR/CP for this process in conjunction with Form TX (different from Short Form TX). The latter method is how I copyright dozens of articles together for one low price. As of July 2006 the copyright fee was $45, which is a bargain to protect your intellectual property. There are other forms available to register different types of literary works. Each form is self-explanatory. If you neglect to complete part of a submitted form, the Copyright Office will contact you for clarification.

One or two copies of the material must accompany your submission and payment. The number of required copies depends on whether the content is published or unpublished. It is recommended that you copyright completed work as soon as possible. It can take up to five months to receive your copyright certificate; however, your work is still protected during that time.

Trademarks—Then and Now

Some business owners protect their company names and logos with a registered trademark. They see the trademark as a long-term investment. They know that their business will be a viable and profitable operation, not a hobby. It can still take a while to start the trademark process, but when it's time, the owner will move forward to complete the work and place an ® symbol after the company name.

That's what I did four years after starting my business. Things weren't the way they are now. Today USPTO online lets you research names from your home or office. In the early 1990s I had to drive ten miles to a metropolitan library with two computers dedicated to researching business names and symbols and a stack of disks that divided the trademark information by last letter.

No one had registered my business name, so I copied the forms and submitted my trademark claim. A USPTO attorney contacted me by mail. He explained minor edits to be made and the deadline for resubmission. I went through this process twice for the trademark because I didn't understand what to do the first time. A few months later, the official notice arrived by mail, and the trademark was mine.

Solo business owners secure their company names and symbols so that no one else can use that particular name or symbol for other products or services. Your registered trademark gives you the right to have an attorney send a cease-and-desist letter to anyone using the same words or symbol. My attorney did this for me when I showed her proof of another party using my business name. The other party's attorney formally replied that the name would no longer be used by his client.

Trademark protection outside of the United States is available, but the cease-and-desist process may have a few more hurdles than same-country rules. Your attorney can explain the details if a problem develops. The USPTO Web site also provides information on worldwide trademark protection.

The USPTO, like the Copyright Office, is adept at explaining all trademark facts through a frequently asked questions section. You will learn what can and cannot be trademarked, the difference between the ™ and registered ® symbols, and more. You can also print registration forms to secure your business name, slogan, and brand symbol.

Trademark protection forms are more difficult to complete than copyright forms, but home-based and solo business owners perform this task every day. Attorneys that specialize in this work are available to take care of the entire process if you have more money than time or believe that an attorney will streamline the work for you.

The current trademark application fee starts at $275. If you plan to submit a trademark request, do so with diligence. The fee is not refundable if you decide not to pursue the trademark after you submit the paperwork.

Patent Protection

Invention property rights, design manufacturing and improvements, and new plant production processes are the main focus of patents. Patents are the only form of intellectual protection for which drawings, usually assigned to copyright protection, are entered to explain the invention's details. Only one type of patent can be submitted online, but that should change in time. Meanwhile, regular mail channels work for every type of patent application.

United States Patent and Trademark Office: www.uspto.gov/web/offices/pac/doc/general/faq.htm#9.

You have choices when filing a patent.

1. Submit the application on your own.
2. Contract an attorney who is versed in patent submission.
3. Use a legitimate patent submission firm.

It is advised that you check and double-check an attorney's or submission firm's credentials before trusting them with the property rights information you've worked so hard to create. Some firms may be legitimate, but many are not. Trusted sources who have successfully submitted a patent with third-party assistance might be able to recommend reputable help.

Strategies to Protect Your Property

Now that you have a general idea of how marketing and security are linked, let's get into specifics that keep your property secured until it's sold.

CDs, DVDs, and Other Technology

Home-based and solo business owners who travel alone throughout the United States to sell their product find the experience to be rewarding, exciting, and tiring all at once. On one end, you must prepare information about your services and create products for sale at the event. On the other end, you must be a gracious host when speaking to potential customers and a stern security officer as you make sure that items don't disappear from sight.

Some tabled items must be the exact product that a customer will receive by mail or other means. Others can be replicas or imitations. The more objects that can pose as the real thing, the better for your security and peace of mind. CDs and other media are the easiest items to simulate. They are valuable property that disappears quickest from a table or display, so you must show replicas. Then you hand customers the real item once the purchase is made.

Here is how to create CD imitations.

1. Collect disks that contain no important data. This includes free trial disks from other companies and disks distributed free of charge at retail and postal outlets. Do not use blank CDs that you've purchased. That wastes your money and depletes a costly product.
2. Create labels similar to the ones placed on your genuine CD products. If these labels are not made in your office, ask the label supplier to provide you with extras. Place the labels onto the replicas.
3. Place the imitation disks into jewel cases to simulate what clients will receive when making a purchase. This step is not mandatory, but do so if you believe that presentation encourages sales.

4. Apply a price sticker directly to the CD label. It will identify the disk as an imitation so you don't sell it unintentionally.
5. Write an "S" on the label using a marker color that's easy to detect. The letter "S" identifies the disk as a sample. Use another letter if preferred. This label marking serves as double protection against selling the product in case the price sticker is removed.

This process also works to protect genuine DVDs and VHS tapes, with minor changes. Storage boxes that house DVDs need not be filled. Simply insert a label into the storage box's outer transparent cover. Blank or broken VHS tapes act as imitations inside of a VHS sleeve. Mark and sticker both in the same format as CDs. An audio-tape (cassette) replica includes its own label on the cover and markings that brand it as a sample.

No one needs to touch the real product until a sale is under way or completed. Products containing genuine data are kept under or behind the table, out of customers' hands. Still, be careful of how you handle the real thing. Some prospects are brazen, walking behind your table or display to rifle through the box of genuine goods when your attention is turned elsewhere. Such actions show that security will always be an issue no matter what controls are put into place.

My products are displayed on a side table that attendees view before and after my seminars. At the end of my talks, I announce that items for sale can be viewed on the table, but purchases must be made through me. Many people purchase, and others have questions. Fifteen minutes after one of my presentations ended, the room was empty, and so was the table. Every imitation CD and DVD was gone. If any had been genuine media, I would have been annoyed at myself for leaving products unattended. The genuine CDs and DVDs were under the main table in front of me. The table samples were Internet access disks received by mail and taken from postal centers where the disks are plentiful. I began to wonder if my closing remarks encouraged attendees to take the tabled items, but I recalled being very specific about buying directly through me. This security system has helped me to market without the stress of manning a table while speaking with people who hear my presentation.

Security is needed for nonspeakers as well. For example, you may host a table display at a chamber of commerce event or another gathering on land or sea. A conversation can become so intense that you suddenly lose track of table products. No matter what setting or types of people attend, there are times when items will disappear. Even if products clearly state "do not take," things somehow get lost. But the problem is lessened by displaying imitations rather than genuine goods.

Protecting valuable media is easy. Create replicas to show customers what's for sale, and then present them with genuine products when they're ready to buy. Now you can display and sell in comfort.

Books, Booklets, and Other Matter

Everyone wants to read parts of a book before they buy or don't buy it. That's what's so great about today's bookstores. They let browsers read everything in the store, curl the pages, spill coffee and crumbs within publications, and then leave the store without a single purchase. But you're not a bookstore. You create booklets and other publications that fit within a certain niche category, so what you sell is information that can't be found anywhere else. This fact allows you to keep some, if not all, of your materials under wraps before it is sold. It may seem difficult to do, and it's obviously difficult for browsers to comprehend. The way in which browsers seem to read all the text within your publications and then quiz you on the contents before walking away empty handed is a major reason why home-based and solo business owners rarely display their products in the open. They'd rather sell such items from the comfort of their offices. But there are times when events lend themselves to additional sales, so security precautions are needed to show printed matter without letting everyone use your display as a library or bookstore.

What about customers who buy your material and return it after obvious signs of duplication? Not all customers do this, but it does happen. There's no law that says you, as a company that produces unique information, must carry a full refund policy. In other words, your policy can state one of the following:

- No returns
- No returns after fifteen days
- Restocking charge of (percentage) for all returns

Many customer service experts say that the more liberal the return policy, the more apt customers will be to buy. However, not all businesses can follow these rules, especially if what you sell is unique to the marketplace. Look at the return policies of other industry participants. Do they offer full refunds? If so, take a closer look at what they sell. Is it similar to your products? Be sure to compare your findings on a balanced ratio. For example, it's customary for a major bookstore to offer customers full refunds. If you sell your own books within a company that does not function as a bookstore, you do not have to offer customers a full refund.

One of my companies does not allow returns because the printed materials, CDs, and other products are so specialized that refunds are not an option. My catalogs and Web sites explain, very specifically, what is contained in each product so that customers can make wise choices. Customers are encouraged to call the office for additional information and to place their order by phone instead of in the online store. My no-return policy is the front-runner for the entire industry it represents. Other industry sellers have also decided not to allow returns. Be sure that your terms are clearly stated on the order form, in your online store, and anywhere else that customers view and order your products.

You may think that a no-return policy works against sales, but that's not true. The policy will serve to deter customers who frequently return products from ordering in the first place.

In addition, you'll have fewer return and adjustment problems.

Books

It's impossible to display a partial self-published or traditionally published book, so do the next best thing: Make a maximum of three books available for browsers to review. These books should be ones that cannot be sold because they are bruised or somewhat damaged. Rather than throw them away, such books are useful to sell the good stock. If someone wants to see a book and all three are in browsers' hands, announce to all that others are waiting to view the books and that you have fresh copies available for purchase.

Another option is to sell the book on-site but not bring it with you. One-person businesses with more than books for sale often bring only the products that have the highest margin for revenue. Books seldom fit that category. For example, if CDs cost $5 wholesale and sell for $30 retail, the margin is $25. If a book cost $10 wholesale and $20 retail, the margin is lower ($10). In addition, books are heavier to carry or ship and take up more space under the sales table. This is why some business owners leave books at the office, opting to bring one sample and take orders on-site. Offering a buying incentive such as free shipping or a free gift with purchase is a method to boost sales of items not at the event.

Booklets and Custom Publications

It takes many hours to craft materials uniquely specific to one industry. Event visitors understand this and know a specialty publication when they see one. The item is taken from the table, absorbed from beginning to end, and then placed back on the table without a sale. Instead of a display acting as a sales table, it acts as a library. I've seen this many times, and it happened to me until I learned how to secure my property before the sale.

The way to protect your booklets, wire-bound documents, and other unique materials is by enclosing them in clear, flat plastic sleeves or bags. The sleeves are fused on three ends and open at the top. Insert each publication in a sleeve, fold the top downward to the back, and add tape or a sticker to keep the sleeve closed until purchased. This, along with keeping the publications behind the counter with CDs and other media, is a good way to stop browsers from opening and reading items for sale.

There's a method for displaying booklets as your for-sale material outside of sharing the entire contents. Let an empty cover or title page act as a sample. The publication's table of contents is displayed alongside the cover, which familiarizes browsers with the information in each booklet. Browsers may ask why the actual booklet isn't available for viewing. Responses such as, "This setup makes it easier for you make the right buying choices," or "I want to make sure there is enough material for everyone to buy," are appropriate, as they express a flair for customer service and accommodation.

Backup Options in the Office

You spent the week creating books, brochures, and other marketing materials. The weekend arrives, and you carefully shut down the computer as you do every Friday. On Monday morning you start your day by pressing the computer button. Nothing happens. Plugs are checked to ensure connections. You even unplug the hard drive from the surge protector and replug it. Still nothing. Your computer is dead. Even if you had renewed your computer's service contract, there's no telling whether your data will be intact if you can get the machine up and running. Now you're really in a panic. What's the next step?

This scene occurs every day in offices around the world. Large corporations suffer when a computer terminal suddenly does not work. Why should home-based and solo business owners act as though they will fare better? Security is mandatory to protect trade secrets and intellectual property from people who want to take shortcuts, but it's even more critical to protect us from our own negligence. How many times have you said to yourself, "I'm going to get a backup system," and it's never done? The cost of installing backup security to a computer system amounts to pennies compared to the aggravation and time it will take to re-create letters, brochures, forms, and plans, not to mention any data provided to you by clients. What will clients think of you when you tell them about the lost data? They may not have another copy. That's just a sample of what happens when computer security is neglected.

FYI: The Cost of Lost Data. http://gbr.pepperdine.edu/033/dataloss.html.

In 2003 David M. Smith, Ph.D., of Pepperdine University's Graziadio School of Business and Management documented his findings on computer malfunctions in the report *The Cost of Lost Data*. Based on an estimated 76.2 million PCs (including laptops) in use throughout the United States, here is what Smith stated as reasons for data loss:

- Hardware failure (hard drive failure, power surges): 40 percent
- Human error (accidental deletion, laptop damage): 29 percent
- Software corruption (diagnostic program damage): 13 percent
- Theft (more common with laptops): 9 percent
- Computer viruses (Internet downloads, file sharing): 6 percent
- Hardware destruction (floods, lightning, fire): 3 percent

Smith also estimated loss in terms of dollars and man-hours:

- Average time to recover data: six hours
- Average cost for time used per person/employee: $170
- Average cost for outside technical assistance: $340
- Lost production time per person/employee: $217
- Total cost per data loss incident: $3,957

The report focused on companies that "rely on data in a distributed environment." If the figures in the second set of statistics were based on home-based and solo business owners working on one computer charged with securing data for an entire firm, the amounts would be much higher. Loss data not only lowers the home-based business's daily productivity, it can also end business, permanently. That's the chance taken each day when you work without a computer backup system.

Computer Security Strategies

Admittedly, it's difficult to wade through computer security options and choose backup equipment, but remember: Lost data will end your solo enterprise. The following tutorial will make the process smoother. First, choose the statement that fits your business lifestyle. Then read the situation that matches.

Problem: I need backup for my office computer, something small enough to keep out of sight and that can be transported if needed.

Solution: An external hard drive.

Problem: I need backup for the office computer, but I also need to access files on the road. Some files contain too much data to load onto my laptop.

Solution: Internet computer storage or a large-capacity flash drive.

Problem: I work in a space so tight that an extra piece of equipment will cramp me. But I still need to backup certain files.

Solution: A USB flash drive.

External Hard Drive

My first computer backup system was a piece of equipment that attached to my computer's parallel port. The product, still available today, uses special 250 megabyte disks to house data. Many people continue to depend on the product, as it's one of many types of external hard drives available in the marketplace.

The words "external hard drive" refer to the ability to store massive amounts of computer data on a storage system that resides outside of a traditional desktop or laptop computer. Every computer maintains an internal storage unit loaded with software that tells the computer what to do when it starts up and dispenses other instructions depending on commands transmitted by keyboard or mouse. An external hard drive acts as a second computer brain, storing every file or specific files you wish to save in case the internal drive fails to work. An external hard drive plugs into any computer or laptop for easy access to the stored data. This is what you need to secure your important documents.

Here are the steps to choose, install, and use an external hard drive.

1. Type the words "external hard drive" into an Internet search engine's search box and you'll be faced with more than seven million references. How do you sort through the options? Begin by becoming familiar with the names of manufacturers that make these products. Many of the sites will lead you to manufacturers that want to influence your buying decision. Other sites will be to places that review these hard drives. It's smart to visit review sites to learn which products are preferred by other users. Don't let glowing or scathing reviews influence you completely. A reputable manufacturer, lots of gigabyte (storage) space, and simple-to-understand controls are what you need.

   Many of the review sites provide links to online retailers that sell these products. Click on the links for general ideas about the equipment and pricing. You'll find that, at most retailers, investing in your peace of mind costs a maximum of $250. That's less than a dollar a day. Make a list of the manufacturers and external hard drive models you wish to see in person.

2. Decide which product is best for your storage needs. The basic requirement for today's home-based business owner is a drive that:

- Holds a minimum of 100 gigabytes of storage (250 is more realistic).
- Makes portability easy, especially when transferring the drive to different outside locations or internal computers.
- Easily transfers data with one button or other quick accessibility.
- Includes as few pieces as possible to complete the storage process (stand-alone unit without CDs or disks, etc.)
- Quickly installs onto your computer or laptop through a parallel, serial, or USB port (connection). Make sure the recommended port is available on your computer. If you have to unplug the printer to share one parallel connection with the external drive, this difficulty will retard your use of the drive, and your data won't be saved regularly enough.

Most external drives connect through the USB port; so again, make sure one is available for quick installation. The USB ports in some older computers are configured at rates of 1.0 or 1.5, versus today's 2.0 standard. Do not be alarmed if your computer alerts you to its lower configuration. The external hard drive will still work.

3. Choose where to buy your storage product, and make the purchase. Visit local retailers that sell external hard drives. These are office supply and electronics retailers. Try to visit their online stores first, making a note of which drives are in stock and prices.

There are times when online sales are lower than the in-store price. When you're ready to buy, retailers often honor their store's online price or the lower price at a competitive store. If buying from an online-only source is better, select that company only after you have ensured that the return or exchange policy is within reason.

4. Attach the external drive to your computer. When the drive arrives, open the box as soon as possible. Make sure everything you've purchased is included. Read the directions to attach and operate your new drive. Place it next to or on top of your computer's tower. Take steps to save one file or folder. You'll find that attaching and using your backup is easier and faster than the time you spend researching the backup. Soon after, save your entire internal hard drive to the external drive, or save specific information that's too important to lose.

5. Create a backup schedule. The instructions provided by most computers will help you to set up a schedule, in conjunction with your new hard drive, that conforms to your work style. Consider weekly backups on Friday afternoon if daily backups are too tedious.

These are the files and folders that are critical for home-based and solo business owners to secure on an external hard drive.

- Software that operates Web site and/or blog
- Letters and other correspondence

- Financial software and documents
- Postcards, newsletters, e-books, and other publications
- Articles, booklets, speeches, and other intellectual property
- Contracts and clients' files

You've moved from working with no security to installing a system that will become habitual every week. Think about all the man-hours you'll save retrieving your work if anything happens to the main computer. Now reward yourself by doing something or going somewhere that makes you happy.

Internet Computer Storage and Access

What if a fire occurred in your office, destroying both your main computer and external hard drive? All data would be gone, with no chance of recovery. An alternative to having an external hard drive in your office is to back up your data using an Internet-based backup system. There are companies that secure your data and give you access to the same data outside of the office.

Add to this the fact that everyone based in a home office doesn't solely work at home. Many businesspeople travel thousands of miles each year. Having access to client information while on the road is usually easy, because the client already has all files in his office. But if you need access to your own work while traveling, that can pose a problem, especially if you neglect to bring the external hard drive attached to your main computer. Additionally, laptop computers are

often targeted by thieves who watch your every move. You can take steps to be one jump ahead of criminals, but a single misstep or distraction may separate you from your laptop. The situation is worse if the laptop contains sensitive information. That's why many solo owners don't load financial and other secretive data onto their laptops. Instead, they use Internet options that give them access to critical data.

Data Option 1: Backup

Internet-based data storage firms specialize in backing up your computer files on their servers, transferring all files or the files of your choosing safely and securely until you change the contents or retrieve the data from anywhere in the world.

Does the thought of placing your most valuable content onto another company's servers make you nervous? You're not alone, but thousands of solo, small, and large companies use these services every day. Firms that protect your data make sure it's safe from attack and convenient to access by:

1. Backing up your data on multiple servers in case one incurs problems.
2. Scanning every file added to their servers for viruses and other data-eating worms.
3. Encrypting your content so that no one can read the data except you.

Most services let you back up data daily or on a schedule that's best for you. Many offer backups on a free trial basis before you invest in the service. After that there is a fee, but it is affordable and usually paid monthly. These data security firms make backups easy by offering one-click services to back up your material.

Data Option 2: Access

Another option lets you access your office computer while on the road, letting you view and work with any file or folder on the main or external hard drive.

Companies that make this connection available let you download their software into your computer. This software is the link that lets you work with files on that computer, whether you are working on another laptop or a workstation in the next room or another part of the world. The connection will work as long as your main computer stays on. If, for some reason, a power outage occurs while you're out of the office, and your office computer does not automatically repower after the outage, you will not be able to access the files.

A data-access system is not to be confused with a backup system.

The companies that make this technology available usually offer a free trial before you subscribe to the service. Data encryption and other security features are included. Make sure you read all information before subscribing to ensure that you are getting the most from the service while on the road or away from the main computer.

Home-based and solo businesses have grown in such great numbers that both these data-protection options are more suited for the one-person office than larger counterparts. Companies offering assistance make many choices available, and the ability to try before you buy is testament to its popularity among businesses that were once overlooked.

USB Flash Drive

FYI: Flash drive definition. http://en.wikipedia.org/wiki/Flash_drive.

Did you ever think that your most-prized files could dangle at the end of a lanyard worn around your neck? That's the beauty of today's technology. External drives known as flash drives are light enough to carry by hand in a backpack or briefcase, and office computers are accessible after downloading software to keep you connected to files wherever you travel. Flash drives act as a feather-light storage option and make lack of security inexcusable.

The flash drive has become an indispensable piece of equipment. Its small size, convenience, and ability to store large files allow certain data to stay secure while traveling. This product is shorter than the average pen and is used to transfer data between computers or protect files in and out of the office.

The most popular flash drive storage sizes are between 256 megabytes and 2 gigabytes. Every office supply store, warehouse club, and electronics retailer sells them, often at sale prices. Product prices steadily decrease as newer flash drives with more storage space become available. Flash drives can be customized with your name and logo to serve as prizes, giveaways, and thank-you gifts.

All computers contain USB ports. A flash drive plugs into a USB port to transfer data from a computer to the flash drive and vice versa. Using a flash drive is much easier than attempting to network two computers just to send one or two files to the other.

As we've seen, marketing and security work together to keep your business strongly represented and protected against intrusions and interruptions, whether by mistake or on purpose. Marketing cannot function properly without a full serving of security. Make sure that both parts are monitored and updated to maximize productivity.

09 Gifts and Other Incentives

Now that you've learned how marketing and security complement each other, perhaps the concept of gifts, incentives, and marketing won't be a big stretch to your imagination. Marketing activities motivate clients to buy from you and to recommend your products and services to their personal and business associates. Marketing is also based on the steps you take to develop and manage relationships with clients and others in the marketing pipeline. The process is similar to tending a garden. You till the land, buy and plant seeds, water and nurture the space, and weed and talk to it occasionally. In the end you hope to build a beautiful patch where one didn't exist in the past. This chapter focuses on the process of watering and nurturing.

Gifts and other incentives work to secure loyalty and trust. Many companies, including your competitors, do little to create allegiance. They collect money, say "thanks," and immediately end the relationship. The negligence is the same online. No card, no reminders, no follow-up whatsoever. No wonder buyers go to other sources when it's time to purchase similar products.

Your strategy will be different from all others. Prospects who subscribe to your e-newsletter will receive, by e-mail, a keepsake list of the top-fifty ways to benefit from what you sell. Clients who purchase from you receive handwritten notes expressing your appreciation. Customers who have invested money in your products and services receive an end-of-year gift, depending on the amount they've invested. Some will receive a gift card (also called a reward card), others get an edible gift, and another group receives complimentary consulting help by phone. These are examples of gifts and incentives that thrill clients, convincing them to keep buying and referring others to your brick-and-mortar or virtual door. Such items are beyond affordable and necessary—they're priceless in their ability to create business opportunities and profits every month of the year. Your plan to find and distribute gifts and incentives when required will make your business shine.

How Incentives Increase Business

Sears continues to be one of my favorite stores. It may not be high on another person's list, but a Sears' salesman was the first person to send me a thank-you note for buying an appliance. It included his business card. I'm sure the note was part of the job's requirement, but those few words of appreciation started a relationship that continues today. It acted as a return incentive. There are products I'll buy only at Sears because of that note, and I continue to receive one each time I buy a new appliance.

That card was my introduction to postsales service, years before I considered starting a business. Its influence led me to include a handwritten appreciation note with each order mailed to my customers, as detailed in chapter 3. At the end of my first year in business, I wanted to express my client appreciation with something that accompanied a holiday card. I searched for an item of value that wouldn't strain my budget and found a West Coast company that sold solid milk chocolate boxes. The box lid was also chocolate, and inside the box were espresso beans dipped in chocolate. My clients would appreciate the product even as they ate the entire gift. I ordered thirty boxes and wrapped the outside packaging of each with a bow.

Twenty of the clients called to rave about the gift. They were so delighted that they asked me to send the same chocolate box to many of their clients. I placed an order for 150 more, shipping them before the holiday. I could not have guessed that my appreciation gift would act as an incentive for my own customers. My quarterly sales were more profitable, and I added new clients to my roster, right in time for the New Year.

Each year a good friend who owns a retail gift shop explores new methods to clear out old merchandise. He reads gift trade magazines and attends business shows to learn how retailers worldwide get rid of slow sellers. One winning strategy lets him use the old merchandise as a sales incentive. He puts several products in small and large bags, placing the bags on a table monitored by an employee. The bags are cinched with a ribbon or staple so no one can see what's inside. Customers purchasing a specific dollar amount of store merchandise receive a bag of goodies. Small bags are for $40 to $74 purchases, while larger bags are for $75 or more in sales. Customers who purchase less than $40 also receive one gift contained in a small pouch. The event is held at different times of the year so that customers don't know when it will occur. This incentive creates a frenzy of in-store activity, acts as a magnet for new customers to come in and shop, and clears out slow-moving products just in time to stock shelves for a new selling season.

Another friend does the same thing, but with an Internet twist. She's a retailer who publishes a highly successful online newsletter filled with gift-giving ideas that lead readers onto her Web site to see special and everyday gift assortments. There is no walk-in store, so this retailer uses her e-newsletter as an incentive. One contest instructs readers to e-mail her when they open the newsletter. The first subscriber who sends an e-mail stating that they opened the publication wins selected merchandise, which is mailed directly to their location. She receives hundreds of e-mails, all from readers who hope to be the winner. Beautiful containers, plush animals, and other brand-new merchandise are mailed free of charge for personal use or resale within the winner's store.

Products lead the pack when it comes to incentives. I've watched television shows that reveal the enthusiasm expressed by cosmetic representatives who receive costume jewelry from their managers at monthly meetings. The jewelry may cost $5, but to a representative who's sold $500 of cosmetics, receiving another bauble is reward in itself.

Don't dismiss service-based gifts and incentives. Like the online retailer, you may need to use an out-of-the-box twist to inspire clients. Consulting services are popular and can be offered to customers whom you consider as VIPs or others

just below that designation. Maps may not seem like an exciting incentive, but one that tells the history of baseball or another sport, along with the location of every ballpark in the United States, is worth gold to an enthusiast. A golf map is an item Roger Green might consider giving to his golf clients. Anyone who loves the sport would be thrilled to receive one.

How Incentives Aid Your Plan

↘ *Incentive* magazine: www.incentivemag.com/incentive/images/05-incentive-study.pdf. www.incentivemag.com/incentive/images/05-facts-report.pdf.

Do you believe that sending appreciation gifts to loyal clients will increase sales? Many companies believe that appreciation gifts work. In 2005 the Center for Concept Development, Ltd. conducted a survey for the Incentive Federation. It revealed the popularity of gift giving to customers, employees, and representatives. Here's the list of products ranked most popular as consumer incentives.

1. Gift certificates
2. Electronics (cameras, telephones, etc.)
3. Plaques and trophies
4. Watches and clocks
5. Apparel
6. Food and beverage

It makes sense that gift certificates reign as

the most popular product. They enable clients to choose exactly the gift they want; you don't have to worry about making the wrong selection. In addition, gift certificates are acceptable when you're not sure what to buy.

Incentive magazine's Gift Certificate 2005 Facts Report showed what large and small businesses consider before using certificates as gifts. Of all respondents:

- 29 percent had an annual gift certificate budget of $1,000 to $4,999.
- 34 percent spent $25 to $49 per recipient.
- 44 percent used certificates as business gifts, and 18 percent used certificates to start or maintain business relationships.
- 72 percent considered a gift certificate incentive program as easy to manage, and 68 percent appreciated its broad appeal.

Any gift or incentive program is easy to operate as long as you maintain a checklist or database management program to track revenue acquired from each customer. Keeping your checklist or database management program updated monthly lets you know how much merchandise is needed for your program.

Motivational Events and Ideas

When thinking about the timing of incentive giving, the first month that may come to mind is December. That's when trinkets of all sizes and styles are traded. But that's not the sole time of year that items are purchased. I bought my appliance from Sears in May, so it wouldn't have been

smart for the salesman to wait for December to send me a thank-you note. You'll find the same to be true in business. There will be reasons to send a client or another person a token of appreciation, such as:

Birthdays. When collecting customer information, ask for the client's birth month. The day is not important because your birthday card, coupon, or small gift is sent at the beginning of the month. It lasts all month long as a reminder of your appreciation. Few companies show gratitude in this manner, so there's room to outshine everyone in your industry.

Referrals. Clients express their loyalty and trust when they recommend your products and services. It's an act that should be rewarded. Ask customers how they learn about your company so the correct party benefits from the referrals. Something small, such as a box of truffles or gift card, along with a handwritten note, is appropriate. What you send depends on what you sell.

Contests. Earlier in this chapter you learned about a woman who uses a contest as motivation to open her online newsletter. That's one incentive example. Others include in-shop contests to increase store traffic and inventory turnover and radio partnerships that award prizes to listeners.

Productivity. Incentives encourage everyone who represents your business on a commission basis to sell more within a certain time frame. Additional quantities may be purchased by existing customers, or the reps may elect to find new clients who will benefit from the item or service. In all cases the incentive must match the revenue. No one is eager to receive steak knives if they sell $7,000 in merchandise.

Anniversaries. Your database management software is capable of logging any type of information required, and that includes the month when a client made his first purchase. Sending anniversary gifts is appropriate in this situation, especially for leased items and recurring bills for maintenance and other service.

Good and bad news. Did a client or spouse recently give birth? Did she win an award? Is the client's industry under investigation because of another business? Cards, small gifts by mail when appropriate, and personal phone calls act as incentives. Most companies only make contact when there's something new to sell or when a bill is overdue. Showing support during positive or unfortunate events elevates your relationship to ally rather than just a salesperson. It's a gesture that goes beyond service.

What should you spend for incentives and gifts? As a small business owner, naturally you want to keep as much profit as possible, because that's what heightens your success. You can stay focused on your financial goal and still buy a valuable incentive for customers at the same time. For example, if a customer has purchased $100 in merchandise, you may elect to spend between 3 to 7 percent of that total on a gift. That amount might seem small, but there are more than pens and pencils that fit within that price range. When attending trade shows and reviewing advertising magazines, you'll see customized notepads and books, soft carrying cases, desk accessories, edible products, and more. Best of all, each item can be packaged to make a great presentation and appear to be worth a lot more than its cost.

Earlier I mentioned chocolate boxes filled with espresso beans that I gave during the holidays to corporate clients. They not only spent hundreds of dollars with me during the year, but some also ordered that same gift for their clients. This shows how your choice of gift sometimes pays for itself, turning an incentive into a profitable investment.

When I began selling products at business and consumer shows, I wanted on-site customers to take something with them as a reminder. That gift was a four-by-six-inch, fifty-page notepad. It stated, "Thanks for your order" at the top and was customized with my business name, address, and telephone number at the bottom (Web sites and e-mail addresses didn't exist). Extras pads that weren't distributed at shows were sent by mail to customers who ordered a certain amount of products or services that year, along with a personalized pen. I chose not to send an edible product because a usable item would stay in front of each person longer than an open-and-eat gift.

As the years progressed I continued to search for something new and different that was useful in an office or on the road, whatever qualified as clever and beneficial. One product sent to clients

SoloBusinessMarketing.com
Member, Marketing Care Club – 2008

Members receive a complimentary thirty-minute consultation per month with Shirley Frazier to discuss business problems and solutions.

By e-mail:
sbmc@solobusinessmarketing.com. Subject Line: SBMC 2008.
By telephone:
(201) 555-2729. Mention your club membership.

Thirty minutes per month. Unused minutes cannot be combined or carried over. All questions and answers may be used to create print or audio products. Nontransferable.

Expires 12/31/08. Value $3,000.00.

was an eyeglass case. It sounds bland, but these cases resemble miniature purses. Colors in swirl, circle, and croco patterns adorned each case, and the soft fabric lining could house a pair of eyeglasses, sunglasses, or any item that fit within the case. Male clients received the same item in gender-pleasing patterns.

Another group received a card initiating them into a members-only club where they were allowed to call my office for either a six- or twelve-month time frame to ask questions regarding their businesses. The business-card-size membership card included instructions for use, conditions, expiration date, and value. The last part is very important so that clients understand the cost of service.

Such an incentive is well within your budget. This card was made using business card stationery sold in office supply stores. When clients

call for consultation, the questions and answers boost your marketing campaign to sell more services. Restate the problem and solution in whatever format you choose: Web site FAQs, e-newsletter format, or proprietary information added to print literature available for sale. This proves that your thirty-minute consultation is time well spent, turning the session into another piece of marketing expertise.

Where to Find Gifts and Incentives

You may think that the ideas I've mentioned fit perfectly into your marketing plan, but there are still other incentive items you can consider. Thankfully, there is an entire industry dedicated to incentive marketing for you to explore. And since home-based and solo business owners can't travel around the world in search of the perfect incentive gift, this chapter examines four sources of incentive products, most of which can be accessed from your office chair. One of them is right to create and strengthen client connections.

Magazines

Three trade magazines—*Incentive*, *Potentials*, and *Promo*—highlight the latest products that motivate clients to buy and employees to be more productive. Each magazine is published monthly and quick to read. The key areas within each publication that help you understand what's available in the incentive market are:

Articles and case studies. Long-format stories explain dilemmas that occur within the business world and how companies find and implement solutions. Many if not all stories focus on large corporations and meeting planner groups layered with management. Still, you will find useful details to transfer into your one-person business.

Columns. Look for sections with quick-to-read ideas that are universal to all businesses. These columns are usually highlighted throughout the magazine with colorful backgrounds that draw attention to the page.

Products. Since these magazines favor incentive items, you'll find photographs of objects throughout each publication, along with contact names and addresses or an insert card to mail for more information. Some favorite incentive items are gift cards, foods and beverages, travel accessories, and electronics. Some items won't fit in your budget; others will seem just right.

Trade magazines aren't available at retail newsstands, but samples may be accessible at libraries that catalog trade publications. Your local librarian should be able to tell you if these magazines are part of their in-house selections. There are two more ways to find these publications.

- Visit trade shows that you qualify to attend. *Incentive*, *Potentials*, and *Promo* are found at incentive-based shows, but they may also make an appearance at your industry's trade shows. Publishers usually make their products available at nonindustry shows to help increase readership. Trade shows you visit may display other incentive-based magazines that are not mentioned here.
- Subscribe online. Magazine Web sites, which are discussed next, allow potential subscribers to complete a subscription request form. The form asks if you are the person who makes buying decisions, how much is spent on incentive purchases, the types of incentives purchased, and from whom they're purchased. If you qualify, your subscription will soon arrive by mail.

↘ *Incentive* magazine: www.incentivemag.com. *Potentials:* www.potentialsmag.com. *Promo* magazine: www.promomagazine.com.

Best of all, these magazines are free of charge to anyone who qualifies for a subscription. That's true for most trade publications. Every trade magazine within the gift industry is complimentary except for one, which is the oldest and most respected, giving it the right to charge a price for the thick, monthly publication. If you review a trade magazine and want to subscribe, do your research. Even if you see a subscription charge within its pages, there is a good chance that you can receive the publication gratis. Call the magazine's toll-free number to learn how you can qualify for a complimentary subscription.

Magazine Web Sites

Each day my mailbox overflows with letters, magazines, journals, and advertising specialty products mentioned in this chapter. Companies promote their incentive pens, pads, and calendars by sending samples to home-based and solo businesses. My daily mail can take an hour or more to review.

Perhaps your day follows the same routine, and you don't want another subscription arriving by mail. If that's true, then reviewing a publication's online content is for you. Many articles found in the printed publication are posted on the magazine's Web site, supplemented by links to product sources and articles from past issues. You can read the information on your computer screen or print the articles to read offline.

Having access to materials from back issues is a plus. The publication's Web site acts as an idea cataloger, storing relevant articles that you bookmark online rather than pile on your office floor. Here's what else you'll find on the Internet site that's not readily available in the print version.

- Program guides that explain how to create and execute an incentive program for reps,

individuals, and corporate clients.

- Links to thousands of suppliers, all grouped by category, selling every imaginable incentive product on the market.
- An editorial calendar detailing the focus of upcoming issues in case you wish to order a print copy that discusses a particular subject in detail.
- Reports outlining why and when to give luxury items, gift cards, certificates, and more.
- Subscription to each publication's online newsletter. Be sure to opt out of any additional e-mail contact that you do not require. If advertisers' e-mails suddenly begin appearing, seemingly as a result of your subscription, you might consider opting out of the newsletter. Continue to review the Web site on your own time.
- Links to other free-of-charge magazine Web sites owned by the publishing group.

Your monthly tasks list should include checking magazine Web sites once each month to learn new ideas and procedures created by companies that use incentives to boost their revenue. Add this to your paper or electronic to-do list.

Trade Shows

The Motivation Show: www.motivation show.com. New York Incentive Rewards & Recognition Expo: www.nyirr.com.

Magazines and their Web sites tell you all about products that promote customer loyalty. Trade shows bring the products up close and personal, letting you see and touch items that exhibitors want you to consider adding to your incentive program. In chapter 8 we looked at these shows from a security angle. But that's not the focus if you're on the buying side of the table. That's the position where you'll find information, fun, and freebies, all waiting for you at shows held throughout the world.

Like trade magazines, trade shows are free of charge. Each show features a keynote speaker who shares his message before the show begins. When the presentation ends, the show doors open, and throngs of eager buyers squeeze through a space controlled by security officials who ensure that you are wearing a badge that admits you into the show. Anyone who's attended in the past knows that the earlier you arrive, the more freebies you collect. Exhibitors tend to run out of samples when buyers spot a giveaway frenzy. The samples are items personalized with the exhibitors' name and logo. A sample is something to take away from the booth after speaking with a representative—although you'll watch some buyers grab and run as if they fear booth management.

Incentive product trade shows sound as though the focus is on getting free samples. That's the activity for a small percentage of attendees. For you, the event will provide a meaningful look at ways in which to reward clients for their loyalty, to thank referrals for new customer recommendations, and to convince prospects to

start a new relationship with your business.

Frame a plan of action before attending a show. Walking in with no plan or budget won't gain you anything except wasted time from the office. Here's what to consider.

1. What do you hope to achieve? Set clear goals, such as finding products within one or several price ranges, learning about product customization options, and speaking with representatives who will guide you through the entire incentive ordering process.

2. What is the average merchandise price you're willing to pay per client? This is determined by calculating how much the average client spent on your products and services. As mentioned earlier, most companies stay within a 3 to 7 percent range of that average. If clients spend approximately $200 per sale, then a reward priced from $6 to $14 is acceptable. Also consider any norms within your industry that adjust this percentage higher or lower.

3. Which companies listed in the preshow directory should you visit? Scan the online or printed list of exhibitors. You will see brand names known worldwide and smaller firms that are unfamiliar. Companies that are unknown but that have names that sound intriguing should have a Web site for further review. Examine the preshow list carefully and decide which booths to visit.

The show operates for at least three days, but in this planning stage, your mission is to make sure you visit specific exhibitors with products that match your needs. Companies not on your list often exhibit merchandise you had not considered. Those booths are bonuses when you're searching for something special.

4. What seminars will you attend? All seminars are generally free, as is the keynote presentation. Review the seminar topics and times. Add to your calendar any lectures that promise to share valuable information. Seminars offer a chance to meet other seminar attendees if you practice your networking skills (see chapter 2).

5. Where else can I go, related to business or fun, while in town? Whether the trade show is located in your town or in another state, you want to make the most of your time out of the office. Web sites, preshow planners, and hotel concierges help you find other places to visit for business or fun. Museums, bookstores, and outdoor events refresh your mind and provide new perspective on problems and solutions. Staying in touch with both sides of your life is important to your health and that of your company.

Be aware of how much material you carry at the show. You will receive a show bag to fill with literature, and exhibitors will also offer bags, but all that paper and giveaway merchandise will become heavy. If you're thinking of bringing a wheeled cart with you, think again. Many shows prohibit these carts on the show floor because they can be tripping hazards. Check the preshow directory to see if wheeled carts are allowed. Better yet, opt to carry only what you want to review when returning to the office, and give your business card to exhibitors to send by mail those materials that you don't need to examine immediately.

Trade Show Directories

Every trade and consumer show publishes a companion directory, available free of charge to all attendees. It lists who exhibited, names the show management staff, describes other shows produced by the group, and it displays advertisements purchased by exhibitors who believe that the extra promotion will increase sales. What's most relevant is the information provided about each exhibitor, including:

- Address
- Toll-free and fax numbers
- Web site and e-mail addresses
- Booth location (important when searching for an exhibitor whose booth number changed from what's shown in the preshow directory)
- Exhibit booth representatives' names
- Description of products and services

This information can be vital to home-based and solo business owners searching for names and merchandise not found in trade show magazines. Some companies focus their marketing dollars on trade show booths rather than buy ad space in publications, so there can be differences in each type of literature.

Directories give you a complete look at the conference. Ordering the directory provides a guided tour of the event when you're unable to attend. In most cases directory copies are available when the show ends. Management offices are happy to send you one for a fee. One of the larger gourmet food shows and a popular craft show each prices its directory at $30.

Before ordering a directory, ask colleagues if they plan to attend a show. One of them may pick up an extra copy while on-site and mail it to you soon after. I do this for industry friends on the West Coast who cannot attend East Coast shows. We help each other in many ways, so we don't charge each other for postage. This gratis arrangement keeps all of us armed with information needed to stay updated within our industry.

I also offer this directory-sharing option to clients in certain industries who, for whatever reason, cannot travel to a show. When cosmetic, fashion, accessories, and furniture conferences that I attend are held in the New York area, I call clients in those industries to find out if they wish to receive a directory. That's part of the customer service I provide to keep our relationship strong, and it's another reason why they won't migrate to a competitor. It's a point to keep in mind when you visit shows or if shows that affect your clients' longevity arrive in your area. What competing firm in your industry provides this type of service to their clients?

Show directories are catalogued in my office library. As the shelf fills, I take one last look at older directories to make sure I've removed any information that should not be discarded. Then I throw away old editions to make space for the new. Be sure to review your directories in the same manner, compiling information from them to create specialty directories discussed in chapter 6.

Incentive Products That Increase Loyalty

Companies exhibiting at trade shows display a wide assortment of products. One side of the show features smaller companies launching incentive merchandise for the first time. On the other side are well-known firms selling items in higher-priced categories. Both groups of gift ideas are important, as all buyers need to make wise choices when rewarding clients. Here are some examples taken directly from the show that I've experienced to give you an idea of what's available and how to evaluate what to buy.

Miniature Foldout Maps

This item is attractive and handy for companies that allow clients to visit their location, and it provides much more than just directions. The map folds small enough to put into a pocket or wallet. When opened, one side contains an actual map of the business owner's area, guiding the client or visitor to the business's address. On the other side, each folded section contains any type of information you can imagine. Tips are printed in one square, a coupon is in another, and a list of important industry dates occupies two squares. Each area is filled according to the business owner's request. Map manufacturers create this item to your specifications. You then distribute the product, which acts as a customized service to complement your marketing plan.

Home-based and solo business owners' offices aren't always accessible to clients. What if you want a foldout map but have no use for the map portion? Companies that manufacture this product will create it in any way you choose. You might replace the map with industry facts and figures or important industry locations. The product was designed to be a map, but suppliers are happy to work with you to create your perfect incentive item.

Movie Tickets

Your customers are tireless workers. They rarely make time for themselves. Casual conversations reveal their love of fiction books, adventure, and getting away from the office. Sending them tickets for a night at the movies, refreshments included, will keep your business on their minds and in turn they refer lots of new business to you.

Every theater chain offers an incentive program to distribute movie and refreshment tickets. The cost of movies today makes this item a thrill for people who enjoy the big-screen environment but not the expense. This incentive package costs less than retail, but to your clients, it will seem as though you've spent a million dollars.

Buying movie tickets has its downside. Not every client will have a particular theater chain in their area, especially if she lives in a rural setting versus a metropolis. If you purchase tickets for one chain, and the closest one is fifty miles away, that may impose a hardship on clients who will either not use the tickets or give them to someone else. Your incentive loses its luster, and so does the possibility of added income or referral business.

Another option is to purchase incentive packages at specialty video-rental retail stores. This may be a better option, as there are more movie-rental retailers than movie theaters. Or you can decide to buy theater tickets for some clients and movie rental certificates for others. In either case, the gift of rest, relaxation, fun, and laughter will make clients very happy to call you a business ally and friend.

Bottled Water with Custom Labels

The recent backlash against buying bottled water may make you hesitate to apply this idea, but remember that your bottles will be distributed free of charge at a worthy event. Additionally, consider pairing your business name with a care-for-the-planet campaign. Donate a portion of any proceeds you receive through on-site and future sales to a charity that's linked with the earth's preservation.

Be sure to display a sign about the charitable partnership next to your bottled water, and promote your sponsorship on event banners. This kind of signage is not typically used by large corporations simply because they are not required to display it. As a solo marketer, posting such signs reaffirms your commitment to the community and the environment, two important considerations in your long-term success.

Edibles

Chocolate, cookie, pizza, popcorn, steak, and seafood manufacturers and distributors create tasty assortments packaged to perfection. Small boxes containing two truffles show appreciation on a small scale when there's no need for a twenty-piece box. Popcorn is delivered in microwavable bags customized with your name and logo or in large pails of ready-to-eat flavors with your company's name displayed on the lid. Firms specializing in combining fruits and foods into gift baskets and boxes are located nationwide. Also consider restaurant certificates for a night of steak and seafood, courtesy of your firm.

Everyone must eat, so if an edible product is selected as an incentive, you'll find a wealth of food products to choose from at trade shows, in magazines, and on Web sites. Most companies offer programs that send gifts directly to your clients or to you for distribution. Before deciding on what to order, you must know clients' preferences—and even their food allergies, dietary restrictions, and flavor distinctions. Which clients eat nuts, and which do not? Is a customer who will receive chocolates maintaining a strict reducing plan? These are some of the questions to ask yourself before sending edible incentives.

The popularity of food gifts keeps this incentive within the top-ten choices worldwide. Select the right gift so you are seen in your clients' eyes as a top-ten business provider. As with the movie tickets, try not to present the client with an edible that he will turn around and redistribute due to dietary restrictions. Make sure your choice will be enjoyed and remembered long after it's consumed.

Electronics

This category is symbolized by cameras, radios, and televisions. But there's more to the electronics group: Desk and alarm clocks, CD players, and miniature radios are part of the category. All are affordable incentives if purchased as part of the 3 to 7 percent sales budget. Disposable cameras make a wonderful gift, and many suppliers allow you to customize the packaging. Some watches also fit this category, although watches may be considered too personal an item for clients.

If electronics fit into your incentive planning, it's best to stick with general-use products for the office or travel. Many exhibitors display electronics at trade shows. Most products are in a glass cabinet for inspection, and you'll need a representative's help for a closer look.

Although the electronics mentioned here are

considered affordable for the one-person office's budget, it is the large corporate clients that these manufacturers court at trade shows. DVD players, flat panel televisions, and iPods are coveted gifts added to prize packages for "the most productive employee," "the salesman with earnings of one million dollars in a quarter," and other outstanding staff members. The incentive product must match the results. This is the same for your clients. The higher the sales investment, the more expensive the incentive gift, within reason.

Internal Revenue Service (IRS) rules state that "you can deduct no more than $25 for business gifts you give directly or indirectly to any one person during your tax year." So while it is acceptable to buy an incentive that is worth more than $25, this amount is the limit you can deduct for tax purposes. The word "acceptable" brings many questions to mind. Is it acceptable to give a client an expensive watch or a camera? Is it appropriate to bestow luxury items? Home-based businesses tend to shy away from such incentives. Clients may perceive the gift as not only expensive but also as an item that, if not purchased, would have reduced their invoice. It's good to know that there are plenty of incentive products that stay within the IRS rules and your own budget.

There's nothing stopping you from buying pens, pencils, letter openers, and other well-known, low-cost specialty products. These items succeed in situations where you need to give away a specialty item but want it to cost as little as possible. Before buying, be aware of the low promotional effectiveness of writing instruments, other than the highly touted brands. I rarely look at the name imprinted on a pen. Do you?

Men-specific incentives include tools, outdoor accessories, and sports memorabilia in product or certificate form. Office supply stores and electronics retailers offer gift cards in various price categories. Three categories to choose very selectively are personal care accessories, smoking products, and barware. Such items should not appear on your incentives list unless you know, beyond a shadow of a doubt, that these are the clients' gift of choice.

Incentive Marketing Ideas

There are times when it's appropriate to tell clients about buying incentives. In other cases no notification is needed, such as end-of-year giving or other times within the year when incentive gifts are dispersed. The Center for Concept Development, Ltd. documented the top methods for alerting customers about gift and incentive programs in its 2005 survey.

1. Advertising (print or electronic)
2. E-mail/direct mail letter (tie)
3. Word of mouth
5. Internet
6. Store displays/signs
7. Newsletter

Businesses that sell in any environment are able to promote effectively using one or more of these categories. For example, a retail store owner uses signs posted on windows and throughout the shop to notify customers about free tote bags filled with merchandise given as an incentive when buying store merchandise. This owner also mails postcards to clients on his mailing list, and if he has a Web site, the incentive offer is posted there as well.

A home-based retailer with no walk-in store uses some of the same marketing techniques, but she can incorporate other ideas. Her merchandise-with-a-purchase incentive is posted front and center on her Web site, and a reminder is added on the secure shopping cart's main page. The signature line in her e-mails announces the event, and postcards are mailed to past clients. Bagged merchandise accompanies this retailer to a consumer trade show where on-site buyers receive the incentive with purchase. This giveaway creates lots of traffic around her booth and encourages more sales. Her online newsletter also mentions the event, and statistics show higher traffic on her Web site and more sales for the month than the same month last year when no incentive was offered.

Service-based business owners benefit from similar techniques and more depending on the industry, collaborations, and ideas gained through networking. An interior designer's incentive offered with the purchase of home window treatments is featured on a postcard or flyer that accompanies services mailed to prospects by a successful real estate agent. Accountants gener-

ally don't need to offer incentives, but those who are just starting or relaunching their businesses might offer a free evaluation. That's what CPA Janet Ross (chapter 1) is considering as she expands. She plans to mention this free evaluation when speaking at luncheon events and networking with potential clients at breakfast and dinner meetings.

Certain industries offer no incentives. Plumbers, pest control, mechanics, electricians, doctors, and dentists are service providers who don't need to distribute gifts of any type to gain your patronage. But these professionals must include basic marketing in their overall business plan to generate revenue.

Incentives bring attention to companies looking for a promotional boost, but offering incentives on too regular a basis may impede your growth. Buyers are notorious for becoming conditioned to waiting for an incentive offer. All of a sudden, gifts that were once popular are no longer special. This is why smart solo businesses offer incentives as part of their yearly promotional plan, not part of everyday business.

Rewarding customers who deliver a generous portion of business and referral clients produces a steady stream of revenue all year long. Choose incentives that match your clients' preferences. Then add their words of gratitude to your print literature and Web site (with permission) to continue the marketing cycle.

10

Six Marketing Ideas for Savvy Soloists

This book has introduced numerous business promotion ideas, and each is achievable by you, the solo business owner. You've reviewed marketing plans (chapter 1), uncovered Internet resources (chapter 7), learned how to market by mail (chapter 3), and read about people who took a wrong turn during the marketing process (chapter 2). Thankfully, there are many entrepreneurs who stay on course. This section unveils six affordable marketing ideas that you may not have considered but, as explained in each story, may become part of your personal marketing arsenal.

Idea No. 1—Using Accessories to Break the Ice

Wholesalers frequently ask me for advice on new ways to market their products. The industries they serve change often due to consolidations, industry turnovers, and economic conditions. That's true for all industries. If you can depend on one thing, it's change and the constant need to stay updated to serve new and current clients.

One of my wholesale clients supplied her customers with beautiful baskets. Each one was crafted masterfully, similar to works of art. No two baskets included the same handle or weaving technique. The wholesaler's warehouse was filled from top to bottom with multicolor baskets in all shapes and sizes, organized on tall steel shelves to easily select and ship baskets when customers ordered.

I called the wholesaler to discuss business ideas, and before we concluded she told me about her plans to visit a grocery store to buy a few items before ending her day. I thought about my supermarket visits and how I bring bags with me for a two-cent credit per bag on each order. Why should this wholesaler concern herself with recycling bags when one of her baskets would not only carry several lightweight items but also serve as a marketing technique?

She considered my idea to be inspiring and promised to choose a basket without a lid to accompany her on the trip. Although this wholesaler was not a regular seller of single baskets, she knew that her community was filled with people who purchased multiple baskets for hobby or business purposes. The basket would surely generate questions from curious shoppers. Cosmetics consultants, scrapbookers, meeting planners, and others in business for themselves or working for large companies were potential buyers, and they could promote the product through word-of-mouth conversations after seeing the basket on her arm.

Both of us believed that this type of promotion within the store would not be prohibited, because:

1. The basket is in use to hold multiple products, serving the same purpose as the store's carryall.
2. The unlidded basket poses no threat to store security. At checkout, it's wise to turn the basket upside down after the contents are removed to prove that the vessel is empty.

3. The wholesaler is being approached by shoppers; she's not soliciting customers herself on the store's premises. Store management wants happy buyers and doesn't mind customers gathering for short discussions about an accessory that won't compete with their inventory.

Before our conversation ended, I told the basket wholesaler to take lots of business cards for distribution when shoppers approached her. Creating a second business card, discussed in chapter 2, might prove beneficial to target this alternative market. We both agreed that standing on the checkout line would encourage more interest from other shoppers and the register attendant, as long as she chose a line with a woman cashier.

You don't have to sell physical products to use the accessory approach. Lynn Colwell, a life and personal coach and owner of Bloom 'n Grow Coaching for Life based in Washington state, discovered that using accessories to break the ice worked better for her than approaching prospective customers with the uninspiring phrase, "I'm a life coach." Lynn acts as an ancillary partner to her clients, providing them with encouragement and action-oriented instruction to keep their goals on track as they pursue their life's work. Here's how Lynn turned a personal accessory into a business generator.

"I don't usually pursue clients through local networking or marketing because I coach by phone and my clients are located throughout the United States," Lynn explains. "One day I decided to attend a full-day program for women entrepreneurs, many of whom I thought would be interested in my services. The vast majority of women attending this program were in the twenties to early thirties age range. I'm sixty, and because of this I sometimes go unnoticed in a crowd of younger women. I wanted to create a way for these women to approach me rather than my joining conversations in which I might not be welcome.

"I had what turned out to be a brilliant idea. I have several Mary Frances purses. She makes handbags that are true works of art. One cannot ignore a Mary Frances bag. Not only are they breathtaking, they are also conversation starters. I chose a beautiful red purse that guarantees lots of attention and headed off for the day. I carried the bag as conspicuously as I could. One by one, women approached me. I stopped counting after ten of them complimented my bag. This gave me the in I needed to ask about their profession. They, in turn, asked me. From there, I gained their permission to contact them about my complimentary coaching call. Those calls resulted in signing two new clients."

Idea No. 2—Suitcase Marketing

When I travel by air to conduct a seminar, I try to maximize my time by checking area adult schools to see if there's time to present a second seminar while in town. The seminar will focus on marketing or creating gifts, two of my specialties. If speaking about gifts, I bring items in my luggage to show attendees how to bundle gifts using cellophane.

Fitting crackers, cheese, cookies, and other goodies in my luggage is time consuming. Each item is packaged separately to minimize damage. This leaves little room for clothing, but I manage to pack everything in one bag. After the seminar I give away some of the goodies to students.

The presence of these food items is the main reason I can expect my luggage to be inspected by Federal Aviation Administration (FAA) officials each time I travel. Many nonclothing items are flagged by their machines, and at the same time luggage packed with only clothes and shoes may be chosen at random for search.

Shirley Says

Stress Benefits, Not Titles

Many solo business owners find that describing their profession in terms of what they accomplish for clients, rather than stating their exact job title, encourages interest and more options to gain business. I've worked with clients who announce themselves as "gift retailers" at networking functions. That designation tells listeners nothing about the benefit to their personal or professional lives. Gift retailers do more than sell gifts. Their products establish relationships between multimillion dollar companies or firms that desire to reach that sales level. It's that type of benefit that networkers need to hear when you're asked, "What do you do?" Creating a sentence that tells the benefit of your product or service provides a boost to your marketing strategy.

This is where my marketing skills move to a new level. I add two things in my suitcase before it's closed for travel: 1) a handwritten note posted on legal paper, and 2) business cards. The white paper lies flat on top of the luggage contents. One message states:

If looking in luggage is not the profession for you, perhaps a career in gift basket design will be more rewarding.

My Web site holds all the answers to start a successful and profitable business. You have my permission to take a business card posted at the bottom for yourself, a friend, or family member.

Wishing you the best that life offers,

Shirley Frazier

My message is not written to encourage airline workers to quit their jobs, but it does offer people an option if they are not living up to their potential. Perhaps a relative or friend has expressed a desire to start a business, and gift basket design happens to be a viable option. The answer is in my luggage, and I'm taking the opportunity to market in a nonthreatening manner. Why not use valuable space to promote the benefits of what you sell along with promoting it with cards, postcards, or flyers?

I'm pleased to say that many business cards have been removed, while everything else in the suitcase arrived at its destination with no problem. There's no way to know how many sales I've gained through this type of marketing, as many orders arrive in my online cart without knowledge of how the client found my site. But as long as I'm able to promote in this manner, I will continue doing so.

Suitcase marketing works whether you're a frequent or sporadic traveler. Your luggage may not always be inspected, but if you must store items during a trip, this option may bring you business in ways you hadn't considered. Here are some tips to make suitcase marketing easy and effective.

- Make sure your message includes an immediate solution that benefits the reader, whether or not the reader is searching for a solution.
- Write your message on legal-size white paper, or letter size if legal paper isn't available. Legal paper provides more room for marketing.
- Use a black, felt-tip pen. If your handwriting isn't legible, select a large, bold Arial or Times Roman font, as some readers may not be able to read italics and other script fonts.
- Clip business cards or another promotional item to the message. Sticky yellow notes that include your business name, Web site address, and telephone number are another option.
- Place the marketing strategy on top of your luggage contents, available for review immediately when the luggage is opened.

New clients are found in the most remote places. If you travel, your packed luggage has the potential to bring you a customer base that's ready and willing to buy. There's nothing on the FAA list of unacceptable carry-on items that prohibits this type of marketing.

Idea No. 3—Using Gifts to Produce Results

Remember the story about the teacup and saucer in chapter 5? Creating that gift was the first time I considered giving a present to someone to make my business stand out. Thankfully, the technique worked, but it doesn't always succeed. I've sent door-opening gifts to Realtors in an attempt to collaborate on thank-you gifts for their clients, to NBC's *The Today Show* to turn my expertise into an on-air appearance, and to a radio executive to try and extend our relationship. All failed miserably. Nonetheless, gift giving should be pursued whenever possible—and appropriate.

There are times when gifts are appropriate and other times when they are prohibited. Pursuing a prospect who works in the private sector (his or her own business, etc.) is suitable, but sending a gift to thank a person in any type of media (television, radio, newspapers, etc.) or law enforcement profession is improper, as it may be seen as a bribe or favoritism. One impression you never want to leave is one of embarrassment. Let networking, books, industry groups, and the Internet keep you updated on gift giving dos and don'ts before deciding how to dazzle the prospect.

Although members of the media usually don't accept gifts, there are exceptions. You must be an industry participant to know and play by the rules. Roz Miller Choice worked as a freelance broadcaster for eighteen years. Like many solo business owners, she succeeded in a number of industries before finding her life's work in New Jersey as a real estate investor. Her story takes marketing to new levels. I'll let her explain.

"Theater was my major in college, but I soon changed my professional outlook when I realized that an acting career might be spotty. So I decided to go into a profession (broadcasting) that I hoped would provide more consistency.

"I grew up in Brooklyn. Surprisingly and thankfully, my broadcasting career began in New York City. This job was with WNYC-TV, a public television station. My job was covering Ed Koch, then mayor of New York, in early 1984. It was a volunteer job, and I was a writer working for no salary.

"After that position I went on to join other New York market TV stations. In the beginning I was a general assignment reporter covering crime, politics, and human interest. I enjoyed the variety. No two days were the same. One day I'd interview Nelson Mandela or the president of another country. The next day I'd report a water main break while standing in three feet of water.

"The broadcasting industry is a hidden job market. You cannot buy the *New York Times* to find an ad for a reporter's job. This industry is all about networking. You have to talk with other reporters to find work. You also hear about jobs from engineers, cameramen, and others in the business. The news director often makes the decision as to who will conduct on-air reporting, and the only way on-camera talent is contracted is through sending a videotape or DVD. Résumés are tossed if not accompanied by a demo.

"I was not contracted to one particular station. As a solo freelancer, it's your job to find your work, so you can be working for three or four stations simultaneously. I wrote news for WNBC Channel 4 in New York while I provided the New York Fox Station with on-air reporting. I cohosted a travel show on New Jersey Network and worked for stations that aired throughout the world, including an assignment as a New York correspondent for CNN. Many reporters hire agents who do the marketing to find them jobs. In my eighteen years as a freelance reporter, I found much more work than an agent could find for me.

"After spending years as a reporter, I decided it was time to produce special shows. To convince television stations and show sponsors to partner with me on a segment about breast cancer, I had to do something outstanding to get their attention. Breast cancer's symbol is a pink ribbon, but instead of ribbons I ordered dozens of pink flowers for delivery to television stations and proposed sponsors. This marketing plan generated many responses, including a meeting with the Susan G. Komen organization to talk about the potential show. My plan faded, but for good reason—a production company and I teamed up to work on a show for the themed restaurant, Planet Hollywood.

"My most costly marketing project is one that led me to my current profession. My plan was to produce home improvement shows, and to prove my passion for this project, I bought a three-family house through a government auction. The house was in major disrepair. A production company worked with me to videotape the renovation project as it moved through the before, during, and after stages. Program directors received the video, which I wrapped in a brown leather-and-suede tool belt containing screwdrivers, electrical tape, a 5-in-1 tool, and other products. This garnered responses from every target. One California television producer was very interested and we discussed creating a show for me. Oddly, instead of the project leading me to home improvement shows, it exposed my talent as a real estate investor."

Roz skillfully employed marketing tactics to attract attention throughout her journey from reporting to real estate. As a freelancer she understood what was necessary to get the desired results. Roz shares one final story about a marketing strategy that I helped her fulfill in the mid-1990s and that continues to pay off today.

"I'm big on saying thank you. A colleague did something very special for me, and I wanted to show my appreciation. I called Shirley. She created a gift basket using a top hat and sent it to him. He received it and was overwhelmed with joy.

"This colleague started a television production company in Manhattan, and it's been successful for more than ten years. He continues to call me to do television production work for him, all because of that gift sent so many years ago. I continue to get business from him because he connects me with that good feeling he experienced opening his gift basket."

Idea No. 4—Specialty Regional Web Sites and Publications

Occasional trips to meetings or for research in or outside of your state allow you to form fresh perspectives about business as you are stimulated by the new environment. The time away can be used in another productive form, as illustrated by this habit I developed when traveling.

First, I search online for Web sites with information on business and casual events. This is a must when going to a conference where you will be out of town for several days. Your main focus is getting the most from the conference, but any downtime should be converted into an opportunity to mingle with people or visit places that aren't readily available at home.

Online newspapers and magazines and specialty Web sites list events at museums, bookstores, and other public facilities. You will also find business gatherings where visitors are welcomed, such as chamber of commerce networking events, dinner meetings, and evening mixers.

➤ *Los Angeles Times:* www.latimes.com. At-la.com: www.at-la.com.

Finding these Web sites takes little time as long as you use proper search engine keywords. For example, if I'm traveling to Los Angeles, I'll first consult the *Los Angeles Times*. The sidebar heading, "Calendarlive," gives readers a breakdown of music, art, theater, and more in a weekly format. It may not be so easy to find business events under the *LA Times'* business section. In that case, type "business meetings"+"Los Angeles" into a search engine, all together and in quotes as shown, and you'll find a listing for at-la.com, an impressive Web site with more information on what's happening in and around Los Angeles in one place.

Second, I search for newspapers by typing "(state name) newspapers" in quotes in any search engine. A list of major publications will appear, as well as weeklies, some of which provide more information on local events than better-known newspapers. This type of search proves extremely helpful in areas outside of metropolitan towns such as New York, Chicago, Atlanta, Dallas, and Los Angeles.

➤ *Today's Chicago Woman:* www.tcwmag.com.

Specialty magazines also make navigation easy when visiting small and large towns. They are often free of charge, referred to as "throwaways," and can be found in town supermarkets, street corner newspaper-dispensing machines, restaurants, conference centers, and airports.

When I visit Chicago I'll consult the *Today's Chicago Woman* Web site, and if there's time, I'll also look for the magazine's hard copy in a dispensing machine on South Michigan Avenue.

Once you review many of these "throwaways," you'll wonder, as I do, why they carry this designation. Some do not provide information that matches your interests, but others supply a wealth of insightful articles, advice, and case studies not found in your local publications. You'll also find a roster of events happening the same time you're in town. Thanks to a regional publication, a profitable business idea might be waiting for you at a local breakfast meeting in a city you're visiting that day.

Consulting these event sources online is part of my out-of-office preparation. However, if I know I'll return to the same area within a year, these publications work to provide ideas for revenue. For example, papers in dispensing machines inform me about community colleges and area learning centers with programs that allow experts to educate the general public about a certain topic. Months before returning to Las Vegas, for example, I scheduled a seminar through a community college and generated $2,000 in speaking fees and sales within two hours. Similar results occurred during trips to Denver and to Portland, Maine. In-class marketing of my reports, CDs, and Web site encourages more sales in the future. This additional revenue was possible because I planned to be in town for one event and decided to reap rewards from

another opportunity. If you have a topic that's presentable in a class format, whether to consumers or business owners, the same approach is open to you if you make research and planning part of your trip preparation.

Third, I visit state chamber of commerce and travel and tourism department Web sites. Chambers usually charge a fee for nonmembers, but if the subject allows for better marketing opportunities, the investment is worth the cost. Each Web site lists events in different formats, but most display an overview of conventions and other gatherings throughout the state. You may not qualify to attend all these gatherings, but if you can get to an event's facility, specialty publications may be available in the lobby with news and other insights about the industry.

Do you still wonder how searching through specialty publications and Web sites strengthens your marketing plan? Here are six benefits.

1. Networking with people outside of your regular circles opens you to ideas previously not considered.
2. Reading where business owners conduct events and seminars provides a new perspective on how to gather prospects and clients to hear your message.
3. Reviewing solutions to business problems uncovers solutions to your own dilemmas and those experienced by clients.
4. Finding new publications lets you share the discovery with associates and clients. This a)

makes them search their memory for similar publications to reciprocate ideas, and b) secures your relationship as a business ally, putting you atop their list of people to contact first when a business opportunity arises.

5. Uncovering competitive companies' Web sites, mentioned in these publications, helps you keep a watchful eye on their strengths and weaknesses.

6. Analyzing potential clients through insightful articles gives you an advantage when you approach them to offer your services.

Regional Web sites and publications aid your business growth, or they work to keep your options strong within a tight niche. Not all locations will have a comprehensive regional site, but each area will have a newspaper with business and/or casual offerings that often lead you to additional listings.

Idea No. 5—Preparing for Your Close-up

Time magazine publishes a special year-end issue of best photos. In 2005 photographs showing the effects of Hurricane Katrina, Pakistan's earthquake, Indonesia's tsunami, London's bombing, Paris's riots, and the wars in Iraq and Sudan topped their list. Best photos also featured the Pope's funeral, Michael Jackson's trial, and the *Gates'* orange banners in New York's Central Park. These pictures remind you of events that are easily forgotten as months pass unless you, your

business, or family members share a direct connection.

Photo galleries are not exclusive to *Time*. Home-based business owners can create their own best photos galleries to post on Web sites, on blogs, and in marketing materials. Have a camera on hand each time products or services are delivered, seminars and speeches are conducted, interns are trained, sponsorships are awarded, and donations are fulfilled. When you capture these memories photographically as part of your marketing plan, you can show prospects and clients how your business impacts others personally and professionally. Digital photos are your first choice, but disposable cameras should not be overlooked if a digital camera isn't available.

Flora Morris Brown, Ph.D., knows all about capturing memorable pictures to boost her business. She teaches critical thinking at Fullerton College in California and promotes educational success on her Web site www.YourEducationMatters.com, but her teaching roots began on the junior high school level. Flora's passion for education led her to open a Los Angeles–based reading and math tutoring program. As she created the program from scratch, Flora knew that it would take a healthy dose of marketing to get the attention her program deserved. Here's how she put her plan in focus.

"I started thinking about a tutoring program when I was a junior high school reading teacher," Flora recounts. "The students needed a concentrated reading program, and I was frustrated that the system didn't create something intensive enough for them. I didn't want to run an entire school, but the children needed extra help, so I decided to focus on a private reading and math program.

"The plan began to develop when I resigned from the junior high school system and returned to the University of Southern California." When Flora completed her Ph.D., she launched the school inside a private preschool that her youngest child attended. Then she moved the part-time program to a church with an educational center.

"The program was so popular that I decided to run it full-time from my home's two-car garage, which was completely remodeled into a space with a classroom, small reception area, and lavatory. It housed a receptionist, teachers, and the students. In time the garage became too cramped. I could not schedule testing for incoming students because testing was being performed in the same space where students were being tutored. A bigger building was needed to accommodate everyone, so I purchased a commercial building in Los Angeles, just fourteen blocks from my home. I thought to myself, 'I have to get more serious to promote a larger program.'

"My marketing campaign started with trifold brochures I made and distributed to the parents at my child's preschool. I advertised in a throwaway paper called *Southwest Wave*. It contained local news, a food section with great recipes, and a church section. The price for a three-line ad was cheap, and it connected me with lots of paying parents. I also succeeded at having my program included on university referral lists. Universities often have these lists for parents looking for tutoring services.

"I met a photographer through a friend. He was a photojournalist, a person who snapped pictures of news as it happened. He encouraged me to write press releases, which became part of my marketing.

"I watched and read the news, looking for dignitaries who would be in town. When I saw something of interest, I called the photographer and asked him to meet me at the event so I could have my photograph taken with the famous person. The photojournalist taught me how to pose and how to help him get good pictures. I had to be assertive when going after my photos. Crowds form around these dignitaries, but I know I must get my picture. Thank goodness this opportunity occurred before today's security concerns. I was able to approach the person and shake his or her hand. Then I'd ask, 'Is it okay if I take a picture with you?' They always approved.

"The photographer and I worked as a team. I would shake the person's hand and tell them where to look. I made sure we were both face forward so it looked like the person was shaking my hand legitimately. The photographer developed eight-by-ten-inch black-and-white photos. I wrote the photo caption, which read similar to 'Dr. Flora Brown, director of the Morris-Brown Reading Academy, greets (person's name) at (location).'

Then I hand delivered the picture to the *Southwest Wave*. Some of the dignitaries who appeared in the newspaper posing with me were the Rev. Jesse Jackson, former Los Angeles mayor Tom Bradley, and California congresswoman Diane Watson."

This local marketing also netted Flora an article in the *Los Angeles Times* and a live segment on a news broadcast. She encourages anyone who wants to pursue this type of photo promotion to work with a professional photographer. "Celebrities move fast through a crowd, so you will only have a few seconds and just one chance to get a great still photo. If you work with an amateur, you may not get the shot you want in a timely manner."

Idea No. 6—Vehicle Marketing

Many home-based business owners, including me, use their personal vehicles as rolling billboards. It's a popular method to market while on the road. Anything from a business name to Web site address is fair game to advertise, depending on the information targeted for marketing and the space required for the message. It's an idea that large corporations and radio stations take one step further by enveloping buses and vans in one gigantic ad. Even the vehicles' windows are coated on the outside, but riders see no trace of it on the inside. One-person businesses, for the most part, haven't elected to spray coat their vehicles in this manner, but there are numerous options for effective marketing while we travel.

I owned a minivan when I began my business. It ensured plenty of room for my gifts as I traveled to corporate presentations and trade shows. My first vehicle sign was made by an office supply company selling its products by catalog. The sign was magnetic (similar to what plumbers, electricians, and real estate agents still use today), placed on the driver's door just below the window. Its white background allowed the black lettering of my company's name, slogan, and telephone number to stand out.

Before buying the sign, I consulted with an attorney to determine if this type of advertisement put my company in jeopardy if an accident occurred. He assured me that any lawsuits would be of a personal nature, not business, because the vehicle did not carry commercial license plates. This is a question to ask your attorney if you choose to place a sign on your vehicle; your region may have different laws and statutes.

I remember feeling self-conscious the first time the sign appeared on the van. People stared at me while waiting at a red light. After a few weeks, telephone calls arrived asking about my products. Some callers said they saw the information on my car sign, so it was working as a promotional tool. More calls and sales resulted in additional income. Years passed, and the van decided to cease operation. Another car took its place, and I needed a new sign.

A visitor on a small business Internet message board mentioned a plastic sign he used on his car. It clung to the inside back windshield, allowing anyone in back of or passing the car to see his message. This seemed to be a sturdy, more weatherproof product than a magnetic sign. I searched the Web and found a supplier of clear, plastic advertising signs, also known as decals, that adhere easily to a vehicle's clean windshield. The sign's background color was clear, but the customized phrase was written in black and outlined in white. I purchased two decals in the late 1990s for under $40. The decals grip sturdily and won't move as long as the entire plastic is pressed onto the window. The product is strong enough to withstand rough handling and is as light as a feather when held in your hand.

I've placed one sign inside my car, where it stays in place unless I move it. The other sign is reserved for use in rental cars. It folds easily, and I place it in a luggage pocket. When I arrive at the rental car lot, I place my advertising sign on the back windshield. If I'm given a car with a tinted back window that masks the sign, I place the decal on the front windshield, high enough not to block my view. This marketing approach is repeated each time I rent a car.

Anyone seeing the car on the road or parked in a lot reads the marketing message and Web site address. It's unclear how much the promotion has helped my business overall, as buyers rarely remember how they find a Web site or telephone number. But you may find yourself in a position to talk about your service in places you never considered to be a temporary office, such as malls, car washes, and ferries transporting people and cars. People will stop you in parking lots to learn about your business because of the promotional decal. This has happened to me numerous times in supermarket and mall lots. Women inquire about my services for their firms and friends who own businesses.

The sign is your business's introduction. Keep other items on hand for distribution to interested parties, such as brochures and business cards. Carry a notepad for writing names, telephone numbers, and notes about people; this will make return calls easier. Most people who talk with me do not carry their business cards—though they should if truly in business—so I must write down the details.

One more important tip: Before you place the order, I suggest you take several days to consider the message written on your sign. An effective message or slogan must be easy to read at a glance. The decal itself only holds a specific number of letters within two rows, so long messages won't do. I chose to broadcast a three-word slogan on the top line and my Web site address on the bottom. It took several days to finalize my decision. I posted my ideas on an office wall to help make the right choice, and I'm still proud to place the sign in vehicles I own or rent.

This mobile promotional method effectively spreads the word about your business, and the price fits your budget because you're already on the road. Home-based and solo business owners can easily add this type of marketing to their plan.

Time to Put Your Plan to Work

The task of marketing seemingly required a team of employees to complete. That myth is finally laid to rest. You now know that the task is manageable on your own with the exception of sporadic assistance from helpers whom you direct to finalize large mailing campaigns. Marketing techniques you select from this book will effectively put your business front and center within your chosen industry. You will implement some ideas frequently because of the high success rate each time they are launched. Other concepts introduced here may provide a promotional boost when attracting a new audience. Most of all, it's up to you to create a marketing plan, revise it, and launch the project to bring buyers to your front door—physical or virtual.

In Summary

We've covered a lot of ground in this book. Here are highlights from each chapter to jumpstart your own home-based business road map.

The marketing plan.

❏ Plan a course of action for your business success by developing a written plan.

❏ Examine area statistics, client lists (if available), current and future industry trends, and your long-range goals.

❏ Review your plan periodically to stay on track and also to change and update your goals.

Solo marketing basics.

❏ Document all information to be placed on business cards, and double-check spellings before printing.

❏ Choose from a variety of business events, held during the day or evening, to meet like-minded people in casual environments.

❏ Meet clients at public meeting places when getting together at your home workspace is not appropriate.

Direct mail marketing.

❏ Determine which types of printed literature make the most impact on your customers:
  - Letters
  - Postcards

- Newsletters
- Surveys

❏ Review junk mail and extract convincing words and powerful phrases to include in your own marketing materials.

❏ Mail handwritten appreciation notes to clients after purchases and referrals are concluded.

Print media marketing.

❏ Create a campaign to write and distribute news releases (also known as press releases) through local and national media.

❏ Learn what the media consider newsworthy to increase your chances for coverage.

❏ Enlist the services of news release distribution services.

Broadcast media marketing.

❏ Media options:
  - General television
  - Cable television
  - General radio
  - Satellite radio

❏ Promotion options:
  1. Enlist a publicist's help. *Pro:* Puts the work in the hands of an expert with media ties. *Con:* Expense may outweigh the results.
  2. Do it yourself. *Pro:* Uses your marketing skills and insight to contact specific media to reach your audience. *Con:* Lots of time is required, which takes you away from other business-building tasks.

❏ Media Appearance Worksheet:
  - Be ready to apply your own makeup if no artist is on-site.
  - For a winning appearance, wear a color other than white.
  - Drink water beforehand to ensure a clean, on-camera smile; eat afterward.
  - Before leaving the studio, ask the producer when to follow up by telephone for another segment.
  - Write the producer an appreciation note after the broadcast.

Technology tools.

❏ Teleseminars:
  - Easy to create live or as a recording burned onto a CD.
  - Choose to interview another person or have someone interview you.
  - Create a script to streamline the discussion.

❏ Directories:
  - Make money from your expertise by creating and selling lists in text, CD, and PDF formats.
  - Compile data about niche industries that would generally take hours for others to collect.

❏ Web videos:
  - Promote your industry knowledge by recording and adding video clips to your Web site.
  - Purchase a video camera, camcorder, or download Photo Story 3 for video creation.

❏ Podcasts:
  - Create an online radio show for customers

who prefer to listen rather than watch videos.

- Look for podcasting firms that make easy work of recording, editing, and uploading the broadcast to your Web site or blog.
- Consider creating podcasts of no more than fifteen to twenty minutes in length.

Internet marketing.

❏ Get your Web site up and running:
  - Select a domain name and register it.
  - Choose a Web site host with templates, e-mail addresses, blogging options, statistics program, and a secure cart to sell online.
  - Review other industry Web sites to gauge their strengths and weaknesses.
❏ Use electronic newsletters:
  - Determine your newsletter's content, frequency, and marketing options.
  - Select a newsletter distribution firm that provides templates, statistics, and support.
  - Monitor the newsletter's success, and continue providing information for readers.
❏ Create a Web site press room (also known as an online media room or "About Us" page), including:
  - Description of products and services
  - Product and publicity photographs
  - List of media appearances
  - List of publications featuring your expert quotes
  - Industry background
  - Celebrity and general customer endorsements/comments

Security concerns.

❏ Intellectual property that may need extra security:
  - Photographs
  - Articles, reports, books, and directories
  - Audiotapes, videotapes, CDs, and DVDs
❏ Know which copyright, trademark, or patent products qualify for government copyright protection.
❏ Install a computer backup system to protect your data from hardware malfunctions.

Marketing with gifts.

❏ Buy gifts for clients to reward them for their loyalty and referral business.
❏ Investigate gift items at incentive shows, in magazines, and on product Web sites.
❏ Ensure that the gift matches the client's level of business.

Marketers' strategy tips.

❏ Treat your product as a travel or shopping accessory for all to see.
❏ Gather and review business magazines when traveling to different regions.
❏ Promote your business with signs and decals affixed to personal vehicles and rental cars.

Above all, be creative, open to change, and willing to accept suggestions and adapt your marketing plan. Use this book as a tool to brainstorm your best ideas. Then move forward with confidence to make your marketing dreams a reality.

Index

adult services, 5–6
advertorials, 34

broadcast media
   after-show follow-up, 81–82
   assistance with, 74
   case study, 77–78
   do-it-yourself, 74–76, 78
   gifts and, 155–57
   key points for, 166
   live vs. taped, 79–81
   overview, 73–74
   satellite radio, 78–79
   worksheet, 75
brochures, 12, 14
business address, 18
business cards
   checklist, 21
   commercial printers, 22
   creating buzz with, 17–18
   distribution of, 20
   exchange of, 23–26
   features, 20, 22
   industry specific, 19–20
   informal meetings and, 26–28
   information on, 18–19
   Internet suppliers, 23
   networking functions, 28–29

   office supply stores, 22
   purchasing, 22–23

client base, 11
copyright, 122–23
custom services, 5, 128

direct mail
   definition of, 36
   incentives and, 35
   industry affiliations, 50–51
   key points for, 165–66
   letters, 35–40
   newsletters, 49–50
   newspaper flyers, 46–48
   notecards, 51–52
   postcards, 40–45
   surveys, 48–49
   U.S. Postal Service, 44–45
   vs. Internet, 31–33
   wording of, 34–35
directories, 89–90
do's and don'ts, xvi–xvii

e-mail, 33, 107

flyers, newspaper
   advantages of, 46

description of, 46
sample, 47
frequently asked questions (FAQs)
CD, 96
consumer and trade, 96
overview, 95
Podcasts, 96
text, 95–96
Web sites, 96

gifts
anniversaries, 139
benefits of, 137–38
birthdays, 138
bottled water, 146–47
budget and, 139–40
contests, 138
customer loyalty, 145
direct mail and, 35, 40
electronics, 147–48
fold out maps, 145–46
gift certificates, 137–38
for good and bad news, 139
increasing business, 136–37
key points for, 167
magazines featuring, 141–42
marketing ideas, 148–49
motivational events, 138–40
movie tickets, 146
overview, 135–36
for productivity, 138–39
for referrals, 138
sample of, 140
sources of, 140–45
trade show directories, 144–45
trade shows, 142–44
Web sites, 142

incentives
anniversaries, 139
benefits of, 137–38
birthdays, 138
bottled water, 146–47
budget and, 139–40
contests, 138
customer loyalty, 145
direct mail and, 35, 40
edibles, 147
electronics, 147–48
foldout maps, 145–46
gift certificates, 137–38
for good and bad news, 139
increasing business, 136–37
magazines featuring, 141–42
marketing ideas, 148–49
motivational events, 138–40
movie tickets, 146
overview, 135–36
for productivity, 138–39
for referrals, 138
sample of, 140
sources of, 140–45
trade show directories, 144–45
trade shows, 142–44
Web sites, 142
industry
independent business statistics, xiii
product business outlook, 4
service business outlook, 11
top ten, xiii
infomercials, 34
intellectual property, 120–22
Internet
business card suppliers, 23
e-mail, 33
frequently asked questions (FAQs) and, 96

key points for, 167
marketing and, 31–33
news releases, 68–70
newsletters, 49–50
Podcasts, 93–95
postcard suppliers, 43
Web site development, 99–115
Web videos, 91–93

junk mail, 34

letters, marketing
    action, 38
    advantages of, 35–36
    closings, 40
    convenience, 40
    enclosures, 40
    experience, 38
    familiarity in, 36
    finale, 38
    flexibility, 38
    focus, 38
    incentive, 40
    introduction, 36, 37
    openings, 40
    samples, 37, 39
    strengths, 40
    tailored for prospects, 36, 38, 40
    types of, 36
logos, 19

market statistics, 4
marketing
    accessories, 151–53
    definition of, xi–xii, 1
    e-mail and, 33
    importance of, 1
    incentives and, 148–49, 155–57

Internet and, 31–33
options, 7, 11–14
photographs and, 159–61
print, 31–32
regional, 157–59
strategy, 167
suitcase, 153–55
technological advances and, 83–97
vehicle, 161–62
marketing plans
    alternate plans, 15
    creation of, xiii–xiv, 15
    definition of, 1
    financial aspects of, 15
    goals, 15
    implementation, 163
    key points of, 165
    objectives, 15
    review and revisions, 15
    timetables, 15
marketing plans, product business
    adult services, 5–6
    company mission, 4
    custom services, 5
    goals and, 4
    industry outlook, 4
    market statistics, 4
    mission statements, 4
    options, 7
    overview of, 2
    problems and solutions, 8
    professional alliances, 7
    regional statistics, 4
    target market, 4
    target region, 4
    web strategy, 6–7
    year-1 objectives, 5–6
    year-5 objectives, 8

youth market, 6
marketing plans, service business
    business outlook, 11
    client base, 11
    media promotion, 14
    mission statement-year 1, 11
    mission statement-year 5, 11
    new service options, 11–12
    options, 13, 14
    overview of, 9
    timetables, 13–14
    web strategies, 12–13
    wrap up, 14
meetings, informal
    location of, 27–28
    meeting overload, 30
    retailers, service organizations and, 26–27
mentoring, 11–12, 13
mission statements
    creation of, 15
    product business, 4
    service business, 11

National Telecommunications and Information
    Association, 32
networking
    breakfast, 28–29
    business cards, 17–26
    dinner, 29
    don'ts, 23–26
    functions for, 28–29
    informal meetings, 26–28
    lunch, 29
    meeting overload, 30
    mixers, 28
news releases
    audience, 62
    determining content, 57–59

distribution worksheet, 71
do's and don'ts, 59–60
editorial calendars, 66–68
editors and reporters, 62–64
fifteen tips for, 64–66
importance of, 56–57
Internet distribution, 68–70
introduction to, 54–56
overview of, 53–54
reporter participation, 60–62
research, 63–64
samples, 55, 59–60, 67–68
uses of, 57
newsletters, 49–50, 109–13
notecards, 51–52

office supplies, retail
    business cards, 22
    postcards, 44

patent protection, 124
Podcasts
    difficulty level, 94
    frequently asked questions (FAQs), 96
    overview, 93
    production procedure, 94–95
    use of, 93–94
postcards
    advantages of, 40–41
    commercial printers, 43–44
    do-it-yourself, 41–42, 44
    function of, 41
    Internet suppliers, 43
    office supply stores, 44
    sample, 42
    U.S. Postal Service, 44–45
printers, commercial
    business cards, 22

postcards, 43–44
professional alliances
    product business, 7
    service business, 12, 14

regional statistics, 4

satellite radio, 78–79
security
    backup options, 128–29
    booklets and custom publications, 128
    books, 126–28
    computer strategies, 129–34
    copyright, 122–23
    external hard drives, 130–32
    intellectual property, 120–22
    Internet storage and access, 132–33
    key points for, 167
    offline, 118–19
    online, 118
    overview, 117–18
    patent protection, 124
    physical, 119–20
    positioning, 120
    refund policy and, 126–27
    strategies, 124–28
    technology and, 124–26
    trade shows, 119
    trademarks, 123–24
    USB flash drive, 133–34
speaking engagements, 11, 13
surveys, 48–49

target markets, 4, 15
target regions, 4
technological tools
    directories, 89–90
    frequently asked questions (FAQs), 95–96

key points for, 166–67
overview, 83–84
Podcasts, 93–95
security and, 124–26, 128–34
teleseminars, 84–89
Web videos, 91–93
worksheet, 97
teleseminars
    costs and revenues, 88–89
    examples of, 84–85
    marketing and sales of, 85
    preparation for, 85–88
timetables, 13–14, 15
trademarks, 123–24

United States Copyright Office, 120
United States Patent and Trademark
    Office, 120, 124
United States Postal Service (USPS)
    newsletters, 51
    post office boxes, 18
    postcards, 44–45
    Web site, 45
user's guide, xv–xvii

Web sites
    blog posts, 108
    creating awareness, 106–7
    creating buzz, 106
    creating customers, 109
    creation software, 103–4
    e-mail signatures, 107
    host sites, 101–3
    incentives and, 142
    increasing traffic, 107–8
    message boards, 107
    newsletters, 109–13
    overview, 99–100

press room, 113–15
review of other sites, 105–6
sample strategy, product business, 6–7
sample strategy, service business, 12–13
select and register name, 100–101
shopping card setup, 104–5
tracking visitors, 108–9
Web sites, informational
blogs, 99, 103
bookmarks, 105
broadcast media, 80
business cards, 18, 23
business magazines, 63
business newspapers, 28
copyright, 120
e-mail marketing, 33, 107
flash drives, 133
incentives, 49, 137, 141
logos, 19
lost data, 129
National Telecommunications and
    Information Association, 32
news releases, 54, 70
newsletters, 109
newspapers, 63
niche marketing, 73
office supply stores, 22, 44
patents, 120, 124

podcasts, 93, 94
postcard templates, 42
radio broadcasts, 93
regional, 157
satellite radio, 78
search engines, 106
subscriptions, 113
target markets, 88
technology, 28
trade shows, 142
trademarks, 120, 124
URLs, 100, 101
U.S. Postal Service (USPS), 45
Web hosting, 99
Web site creation, 103, 104
Web site storage, 101
Web videos, 91
Web strategies
product business, 6–7
service business, 12–13
Web videos
recording equipment, 92–93
software, 91–92

yearly objectives
product business, 5–6, 8
service business, 11
youth market, 6